"By grace are ye saved, through faith *plus* works" is the false doctrine of several legalistic cults and religions of the world today. The book of Galatians was written to combat such heresy and to confirm the truth of the gospel as it is taught in the other books of the New Testament. Your study of this epistle will be more than a doctrinal study. In a very practical way you will be encouraged and inspired to move forward spiritually in the power and direction of the Holy Spirit, enjoying the freedom of your new life in Christ. Multitudes of Christians before you have experienced this spiritual lift. The experience can be yours as well.
Introduction:	

Suggestions for Study:

Bible study can be a very enjoyable experience for any Christian who really wants to know what God has written. Here are a few suggestions to make your study of Galatians profitable:

1. Have right attitudes, such as a hunger to be fed, and an honesty to accept reproof from God.

2. Stay with the momentum of this manual as it moves from the general to the specific, from the whole to the parts. This means surveying Galatians as a book before analyzing its chapters, viewing a chapter before studying its paragraphs, and the moving on from paragraphs to verses to phrases to words.

3. *Think Galatians* as you study Galatians. Don't get sidetracked on other issues, important as they may be.

4. When you are studying alone, read the Bible text *aloud* if this is possible.

5. Keep digging into the Scriptures to discover all its precious gems. Don't be content with studying only the *elementary* truths of the gospel. (See Heb 5:11 ff.)

6. Scrutinize every word and complete phrase of the Bible text. Tarry long over the *strong* words. Train your

1

eyes to see *what* the Bible says and *how* it says it. This is the heart of inductive Bible study.

7. Keep on recording your observations on paper or in this manual study. "The pencil is one of the best eyes."

8. Study as much as you can *on your own* before resorting to outside helps, such as commentaries. The exercises and directions of this manual are intended to encourage independent study.

9. Compare the Bible text of your basic study version with modern translations and paraphrases. The version generally referred to in this manual is the King James Version.

10. Read every cross-reference Scripture verse cited in each lesson. It is very true that the Bible is best interpreted by itself.

11. The various charts of this manual can be used to great advantage. Survey charts show general movements and highlights. Analytical charts are organized work sheets for recording observations of your analytical studies.

12. Keep *application* always before you as your ultimate goal in studying a passage. The order of study is (1) observation, (2) interpretation, (3) application. Avoid a mere intellectual study. Let the Scriptures continually storm the will of your heart, that you may grow spiritually (1 Pe 2:2).

Outside Helps:

Here are some valuable outside helps recommended for your study (see bibliographical entries at the end of this manual):

1. an exhaustive concordance
2. A Bible dictionary or encyclopedia
3. a book on word studies
4. guide on how to record an analytical study[1]
5. modern translations and paraphrases

In analytical Bible study one should *concentrate* on one version of the Bible, and *compare* readings of other versions. Such a comparative study throws light on obscure passages, extends the scope of vision, and excites overall interest in the passage being studied. The following statement appears in the foreword of *The Four Translation New Testament*: "The beauty of the King James must be

---

[1] This writer's book *Independent Bible Study* describes in detail how to record observations on an analytical chart (e.g., Chart R).

supplemented with the clarity of modern language. Perhaps the most effective way to retain the beauty and inspiration of one translation while benefiting from the clarity of another is to study the two together."

The New American Standard Bible is a highly recommended modern translation. One of its main values in format is the printing of the Bible text in a single column on a page. This is valuable for at least two reasons: (1) since childhood our education in reading has been with books of this format; (2) phrases are not interrupted at the end of the margin as often as in a two-column page. This is important for phrase-consciousness.

Parts of Each Lesson:

Beginning with the analytical studies of Lesson 3, each lesson involves the following areas of study:

1. *Preparation for Study.* This may involve such things as reading background passages in the Old Testament, or reviewing previous lessons.

2. *Analysis.* This is the heart of your study. The first exercises involve studying the segment as a whole, and this is followed by analysis of each paragraph.

3. *Notes.* Comments are made on words or phrases of the Bible text, concerning information or interpretation not readily discernible in the text.

4. *For Thought and Discussion.* Practical questions appear here, to help you apply the text to daily life. If you are studying in a group, you will want to discuss these questions.

5. *Further Study.* Subjects for extended study are suggested here. Consider these as optional exercises. The continuity of the lessons is not broken if you choose not to do these studies.

6. *Words to Ponder.* It is well to conclude a Bible study with a meditation of a selected verse in the passage.

BLACK SEA

PONTUS

BITHYNIA

GALATIA

MYSIA

ASIA

Antioch

CAPPADOCIA

Smyrna
Ephesus

Iconium

Lystra

Derbe

Tarsus

PAMPHYLIA

CILICIA

Patmos

LYCIA

Antioch

SYRIA

CYPRUS

KEY CITIES

Antioch near Pisidia ⎤
Iconium   │ cities
Lystra   │ of
Derbe   ⎦ Galatia

Antioch of Syria
Jerusalem
Tarsus
Damascus

MEDITERRANEAN SEA
THE GREAT SEA

Damascus

JUDEA

Jerusalem

EGYPT

RED SEA

The Geography of Galatians

Background of Galatians

A STUDY OF A BOOK OF THE BIBLE

IS ALWAYS HELPED BY LOOKING

INTO THE BOOK'S BACKGROUND.

Typical questions asked here are, Who wrote the book? To whom? When? and Why? Such background study makes us feel more at home with the Bible book, taking it out of the "stranger" classification. Also, it serves as a healthy reminder to us that although the holy, infallible Scriptures originated with God, they were born out of human circumstances *involving people like ourselves.*

After we have completed this study of *setting*, we will be ready to make a general *survey* of the Bible book as a whole (Lesson 2). That survey then is our introduction to the main part of our study of Galatians, which involves detailed *analysis* of words, verses, paragraphs and chapters (Lessons 3—10). This order (background, survey, analysis) is the normal procedure in the study of a book of the Bible. It is the order followed in all of the self-study guides of this series.

For all books of the Bible, some questions of background remain unanswered (e.g., "Who wrote Hebrews?"). We may rest assured that whatever background is necessary for an *adequate* understanding of the Bible text is supplied in that text, whether of that particular book or of another book of the Bible. All other background which is available from sources outside the Bible (such as secular history) we cherish as a bonus, and use to further enhance our study.

Let us see how much can be known of the setting of Paul's epistle to the Galatians.

I. AUTHOR.

The writer is identified in the text as "Paul, an apostle" (1:1; cf. 6:11). Some interesting things are to be said about his name. *Paul*, meaning "little," was his Roman name. His Hebrew name was *Saul* ("asked of God"). Very possibly he had both names from childhood. In his epistles the apostle always refers to himself as Paul. Consult an exhaustive concordance for all the references to the two names in the New Testament. Read Acts 13:9, which is the turning point in Acts for the changeover of designation from Saul to Paul.

Important dates in the life of Paul include the following:[1]

4 B.C.	Birth of Paul (about the same time as Christ's birth[2])
A.D. 33	Paul Saved (Ac 9)
47	First missionary journey begun (Ac 13:1)
49	Second missionary journey begun (Ac 15:36)
52	Third missionary journey begun (Ac 18:23)
56	Paul arrested in Jerusalem (Ac 21:18)
61	Paul's first imprisonment in Rome (Ac 28)
62	Release from prison
62-66	Period of liberty
67	Second imprisonment
67	Executed by Nero

Read Galatians 1:2 and observe that other Christians join with Paul in greeting the Galatian churches: "all the brethren which are with me."

II. TO WHOM WRITTEN.

The text identifies the original readers as "the churches of Galatia" (1:2; cf. 3:1). The other places in the New Testament where the reference to "Galatia" appears are these: 1 Corinthians 16:1; 2 Timothy 4:10; 1 Peter 1:1; Acts 16:6; 18:23. (Be sure to read all Bible references cited in this lesson.)

It is interesting to observe that this is the only Pauline epistle addressed as such to a *group* of churches. Some of

---

[1] Dates in some cases are approximate.
[2] See James Stalker, *The Life of St. Paul*, pp. 17-18. Because of this coincidence, one can quickly estimate Paul's age at any given A.D. date.

Paul's epistles (e.g., Ephesians) were intended to be circulated among churches, even though one church was designated as the original recipient.

Where were these "churches of Galatia" located? Two different views are held on this: (1) the North Galatian View—churches founded on Paul's second missionary journey when he passed through the northern districts of Asia Minor; (2) the South Galatian View—churches founded on Paul's first missionary journey to such "southern" cities as Lystra and Derbe. The latter view is the one held by most expositors today. See Appendix for brief descriptions and defenses of each of these views.

The position taken by this manual is that the "churches of Galatia" were located in the southern cities evangelized by Paul on his first missionary journey. The following suggestions for study are geared to this position:

1. Study the map showing the geography of Galatians (Chart A). Note the locations of these cities: Antioch, Iconium, Lystra and Derbe. Try to fix these locations in your mind in order to help you *visualize* and *feel* the real situations behind the Bible text which you will be studying. ("To visualize is to empathize.")

2. Read Acts 13:1—14:28, which is Luke's reporting of Paul's first missionary journey. Study especially the ministries and events at the four Galatian cities mentioned above. These are the cities where Paul won converts and founded the churches to whom he wrote Galatians. Note: Paul's return trip on the first missionary journey (Ac 14:21-27) might be called a second visit to the people. Observe that as of Acts 14:23, churches in the area were already being established.

3. It is generally believed that most of the Galatian believers were of Gentile background. How is this supported by the following verses in Galatians:

4:8 ___NOT KNOW GOD_____

5:2 ___"IF you RECIEVE CIRCUMCISION"_____

6:12 ___"CIRCUMCISION_____

2:5 (in its context) _____

4. What do the following verses tell you about the Galatian churches, and about Paul's relationship to them:

7

WRITINGS OF PAUL LISTED CHRONOLOGICALLY WITH THE OTHER NEW TESTAMENT BOOKS

BIOGRAPHY OF PAUL	BOOK	AUTHOR	PLACE WRITTEN	DATE A.D.	PERIODS		
					Personnel	Apostolic Literature	Church
	JAMES	JAMES	Jerusalem	45			
FIRST MISSIONARY JOURNEY							
— Interim —	GALATIANS		Antioch	48			
SECOND MISSIONARY JOURNEY	1 THESSALONIANS		Corinth	52	FIRST PAULINE PERIOD		
	2 THESSALONIANS	PAUL	Corinth	"			
THIRD MISSIONARY JOURNEY	1 CORINTHIANS		Ephesus	55			
	2 CORINTHIANS		Macedonia			BEGINNINGS —about 15 years	FOUNDING
	ROMANS		Corinth	56			
ARREST; FROM JERUSALEM TO ROME	MATTHEW LUKE ACTS	MATTHEW LUKE	Jerusalem? Rome	61	FIRST HISTORICAL RECORDS		
FIRST IMPRISONMENT	COLOSSIANS EPHESIANS PHILEMON PHILIPPIANS	PAUL	Rome	61	CENTRAL PAULINE PERIOD		
RELEASE	1 TIMOTHY TITUS	PAUL	Rome	62 —	PAUL'S LEGACY	CENTRAL —about 10 years	ESTABLISHING
SECOND IMPRISONMENT; THEN DEATH	2 TIMOTHY			67			
	HEBREWS JUDE	? JUDE					
	1 PETER 2 PETER MARK	PETER MARK		68 ?	PETER'S LEGACY		
FALL OF JERUSALEM				70		15 "silent" years	
	JOHN 1 JOHN 2 JOHN 3 JOHN REVELATION	JOHN	Ephesus Patmos	85 96	JOHN'S LEGACY	CLOSING —about 10 years	CONTINUING

RAPID DESERTION of FAITH.

1:6-7 ~~_____~~

1:8, 11 ~~_____~~

3:1-5 ~~_____~~ — who has Bewitched you — works a faith.

4:12-15 ~~_____~~

4:19-20 Loving Laboring, Perplexed

5:7-9 — Persuaded from Correct Running — why who
vs 9 — Little Leaven levens the whole Lump

III. DATE.

The epistle to the Galatians was Paul's first inspired writing. (See Chart B for a chronology of Paul's ministry which places Galatians first in the list.) He wrote it after his first missionary journey (Ac 13-14) and before the Jerusalem council (Ac 15). The Jerusalem council was held in A.D. 49, so A.D. 48 may be assigned to the epistle. The epistle of James (A.D. 45) was probably the only other New Testament book antedating Galatians.

IV. SETTING.

The first opposition which the Gentile Christians of Galatia encountered after their conversion was that of persecution from Jewish unbelievers of their own hometowns (cf. Ac 13:45-50; 14:21-23). Apparently the Christians withstood these attacks, for Paul does not refer to such a problem in his epistle. Satan changed his tactics against the Galatians and used Jewish Christians from without (probably from Jerusalem) to cast a pall of doubt over Paul's evangelistic ministry among them. "Where the blustering storm of opposition failed the subtle influences of persuasion had met with more success."[3]

It all happened very fast. Soon after Paul left the cities of Galatia on his first missionary journey, Judaizers arrived and told the new converts that they had not heard the *whole* gospel (1:6-7). These troublemakers taught that salvation was by (1) faith in Christ, *plus* (2) observation of Jewish ceremonies (e.g., circumcision). In other words, the Gentile converts of Galatia were not saved if they had

[3] C. F. Hogg and W. E. Vine, *The Epistle to the Galatians*, p. 7.

not also become Jews. Read the following verses of Galatians and record the various false doctrines taught by these opponents of Paul:

1:6-9 _Distorted Gospel of Christ_

2:16 _Justification by Works of Law_

3:2-3 _Recieve sparot by works of thusan_

4:10, (21) _Righteousness Based on Law_

5:2-4 _Law - Circumcission Necc_

6:12 _Circumcission Escapes Guilt of Cross of_

Also record how each of the following verses identify these false teachers: 1:7; 5:10, 12 _Distorted Gospel_

3:1 — _Bewitched you_

4:17 _Exclude you from flock - Then - devour you._

Why do you think it was difficult for many Jews in Paul's day to accept the doctrine of *salvation through faith alone?* One writer comments on this, "Two thousand years of Jewish tradition were in their bones."[4] What were some of the ingredients of that tradition (e.g., forefathers, the temple)? Read Acts 6—7 to see how one Jew, Stephen, saw the deeper significance of the sacred Jewish institutions, as they pointed to a Messiah not only on the throne of David but also on the throne of the universe.[5]

V. PURPOSES.

Some of the main purposes of Paul in writing this epistle were:

1. to expose the false teachings of the Judaizers who were undermining the faith of the new converts

2. to defend Paul's apostleship which was being challenged by these Judaizers

---

[4] William Neil, *The Letter of Paul to the Galatians,* p. 4.

[5] Stephen was probably a Hellenistic Jew speaking the Greek language and adopting Greek customs. The speech of Ac 7 was delivered to an audience in Jerusalem about 15 years before Galatians was written.

3. to emphasize that salvation is through faith alone, not faith plus law

4. to exhort the Galatian Christians to live in the liberty brought by Christ (5:1), bringing forth fruit of the Spirit (5:22-23)

VI. CHARACTERISTICS OF THE EPISTLE.

Distinguishing marks of the epistle include the following:

1. *Many contrasts.* These will be seen in our survey study of Lesson 2.

2. *Strong statements.* Paul was justifiably incensed over the destructive work of the troublemakers. Twice in the opening chapter he writes, "Let him be accursed." "The Epistle to the Galatians is spiritual dynamite, and it is therefore almost impossible to handle it without explosions."[6] The writer of this epistle has been described as "a man with a brilliant mind, a trenchant controversialist, a fearless fighter . . . a man whose life was 'hidden with Christ in God.' "[7]

3. *Clear distinction between faith and works as the condition for salvation.* The book has been used of God to bring spiritual awakening to such men as Martin Luther and John Wesley. Luther said this of Galatians: "It is my epistle; I have betrothed myself to it: it is my wife."

4. *Classic treatment of Christian liberty.* This is why the epistle has been called "The Magna Charta of spiritual emancipation."

5. *No congratulations or words of praise.* It was not that there was nothing commendable about the Galatians' spiritual lives. The epistle was written under strain of urgency, over a situation of emergency. Paul would have later contacts with the churches when he could inspire them through commendation.

VII. RELATION TO OTHER NEW TESTAMENT BOOKS.

Refer to Chart B and review the chronological order of writing of Paul's epistles. Then study Chart C, which shows groupings of the New Testament books by *topics*

---

[6] R. A. Cole, *The Epistle of Paul to the Galatians,* p. 11.
[7] Neil, p. 89.

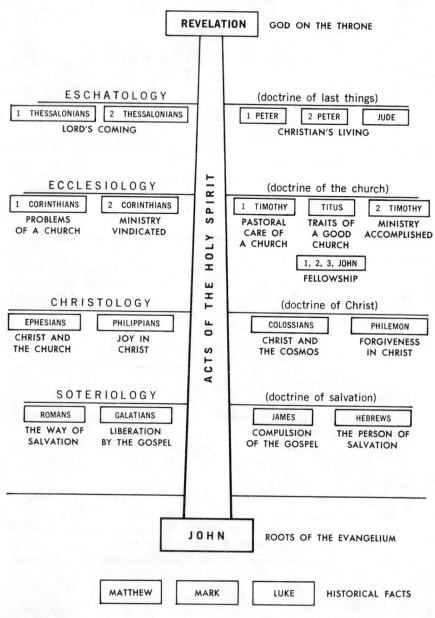

REVELATION — GOD ON THE THRONE

ACTS OF THE HOLY SPIRIT

ESCHATOLOGY — (doctrine of last things)

| 1 THESSALONIANS | 2 THESSALONIANS |
LORD'S COMING

| 1 PETER | 2 PETER | JUDE |
CHRISTIAN'S LIVING

ECCLESIOLOGY — (doctrine of the church)

| 1 CORINTHIANS | 2 CORINTHIANS |
PROBLEMS OF A CHURCH — MINISTRY VINDICATED

| 1 TIMOTHY | TITUS | 2 TIMOTHY |
PASTORAL CARE OF A CHURCH — TRAITS OF A GOOD CHURCH — MINISTRY ACCOMPLISHED

1, 2, 3, JOHN
FELLOWSHIP

CHRISTOLOGY — (doctrine of Christ)

| EPHESIANS | PHILIPPIANS |
CHRIST AND THE CHURCH — JOY IN CHRIST

| COLOSSIANS | PHILEMON |
CHRIST AND THE COSMOS — FORGIVENESS IN CHRIST

SOTERIOLOGY — (doctrine of salvation)

| ROMANS | GALATIANS |
THE WAY OF SALVATION — LIBERATION BY THE GOSPEL

| JAMES | HEBREWS |
COMPULSION OF THE GOSPEL — THE PERSON OF SALVATION

JOHN — ROOTS OF THE EVANGELIUM

| MATTHEW | MARK | LUKE | HISTORICAL FACTS

(e.g., *ecclesiology*, doctrine of the church). With what topic is Galatians identified?

A. Galatians and James.

It is interesting to observe that the first two New Testament books to be written (James, A.D. 45; Galatians, A.D. 48) concerned themselves with the subject of *works*. Each book stressed a different, though not contradictory, aspect of that common subject. James was addressed to the error of antinomianism (from *anti*, "against" and *nomos*, "law"), which said that since a person is saved by grace through faith, works thereafter are not important. (Read Ja 2:14-26.) Galatians was addressed to the error of what might be called *Galatianism*, which said that one is *saved* through faith and *perfected* by the keeping of the law, thus salvation is by faith *plus* works. Stated another way,

Galatians teaches **liberation by the gospel;**
James teaches **compulsion of the gospel.**

This is the comparison shown on Chart C. It is easy to see from this why a study of Galatians made in conjunction with a study of James brings out the stable, balanced New Testament teaching on the place of *works* in the doctrine of salvation.

B. Galatians and Romans.

The subject of works is also prominent in Romans, the epistle that exposes the error of legalism, which says that a person is saved by works. The subject of justification by faith appears often in both Romans and Galatians. (Read Gal 2:16-17; 3:11, 24; 5:4; Ro 3:20, 24, 28; 5:1, 9.) The large subject of salvation is treated more fully in Romans. It has been said that Galatians is the "rough block" of what appears in more finished form in Romans, written eight years later.

C. Galatians and 2 Corinthians.

Much of 2 Corinthians is devoted to a defense of Paul's apostleship (e.g., 2 Co 10—13), because Paul's opponents were stirring up the Corinthian believers by challenging his credentials as an apostle. In the first two chapters of Galatians, Paul defends his apostleship which was challenged by the same kind of troublemakers. If you have already studied 2 Corinthians you will want to recall its *apologia* passages when you study Galatians 1—2.

VIII. APPLICATIONS.

As you study the text of Galatians, you will be continually making spiritual applications to your life and the life of others. This, after all, is the ultimate purpose of Scripture (2 Ti 3:16-17). Some of the *areas* of applications derived from Galatians are identified here:

1. One's salvation. What really are the conditions for salvation which a person must fulfill?

2. One's Christian growth (sanctification). Does this come by self-effort? What is the source of strength?

3. One's conscience. Where can peace be found for a troubled conscience? John Bunyan, in deep distress over his "inward pollution," found his answer in an old copy of Martin Luther's commentary on Galatians. Later he gave his testimony: "I prefer this book of Martin Luther on the Galatians (excepting the Holy Bible) before all the books that ever I have seen, as *most fit for a wounded conscience*." (Read 5:1; cf. Heb 9:14.)

4. One's liberty. What are my privileges of freedom in Christ? Is the church of Christ supposed to be uniform in custom and habit in all respects? Did Paul urge Gentile Christians to act like Jewish Christians, or Jewish Christians to act like Gentile Christians?

Some Review Questions

1. Recall some of the high points of Paul's life. Where does the writing of Galatians fit in here?

2. Where were the churches of Galatia located?

3. When had Paul first met these Galatians? Did he have any part in the founding of the local churches in the different cities?

4. Why is it held that Paul wrote Galatians *before* the Jerusalem council of Acts 15?

5. Why did Paul write to the churches of Galatia so soon after completing his evangelistic mission to them?

6. What was the local setting which brought on this letter?

7. Name four main purposes of the epistle.

8. What are some of the distinguishing marks of the epistle?

9. Compare Galatians with James, Romans and 2 Corinthians.

10. What are some things to look for in Galatians which you may profitably apply to your own life?

14

LESSON 2

Survey of Galatians

BEFORE WE ANALYZE THE TEXT OF

GALATIANS IN DETAIL, IT WILL HELP

TO SURVEY THE BOOK AS A WHOLE.

This survey stage of study is sometimes called the synthetic method.[1] It is like the skyscraper view of a city which reveals prominent landmarks, topography, geographical orientations and associations.

The main benefits that come of surveying a Bible book are:

1. an awareness of what are the *prominent* truths of the book

2. an *involvement* in the book by catching its tone and atmosphere

3. an *incentive* to spend much time in analyzing its parts

4. an *orientation* that will guard against hasty conclusions and lopsided attention in analysis

Keep these benefits in mind as you proceed with your survey of Galatians. Don't let the price of *time* and *work* scare you away from a diligent study of the Scriptures. Bible study is work, but it is enjoyable and profitable!

The suggestions given below represent procedures of survey which can be adjusted to the reader's abilities and resources of time. Occasionally observations and outlines are offered by the manual to help maintain a momentum in your study. These need not hinder your own independent study.

[1] The word *synthetic* is from the Greek words *sun* ("with") and *the* ("put"). In synthesis, one puts together; in analysis, he takes apart. Synthesis proceeds from the parts to the whole; analysis moves from the whole to the parts.

I. A FIRST READING OF GALATIANS.

Aim here to get a *feel* of the book. Read the entire book in
one sitting in a paraphrase edition of the New Testament
(e.g., *Living New Testament,* Phillips' *Letters to Young
Churches,* or *Good News for Modern Man*).
What are your impressions after this reading? Record some

of these. _____

_____

_____

_____

II. A SCANNING OF THE BOOK.

Now go to your basic study version. (If your Bible has
extensive outlining incorporated in the columns, try to
overlook this in the early stages of your study.) Approach
the text, as much as is possible, with an "innocence of the
eye," that is, as though you had never seen it before.

1. How many chapters are there in Galatians? Is there an
opening salutation in the first chapter? What would you

consider to be the concluding section of the letter? _____

_____

_____

2. Scan the entire book for the general content of its
chapters. How do the first two chapters differ from the

others as to content? _____

_____

_____

Which group has more commands: chapters 3—4, or 5—6?

_____

3. What subjects of the epistle have stood out as prominent

thus far in your survey? _____

_____

_____

III. GETTING PARAGRAPH TITLES.

For a longer book of the Bible, this exercise would involve chapter titles rather than paragraph titles. Because Galatians has only six chapters we will start with the paragraphs. The aim here is to identify the main subject of each paragraph without tarrying over any details.

A paragraph title is a word or short phrase taken directly from the Bible text which represents a main subject of the paragraph. The sum total of paragraph titles is not intended to be an organized outline. The exercise of getting the paragraph titles is more important than the titles themselves.

PARAGRAPH TITLES   Chart D

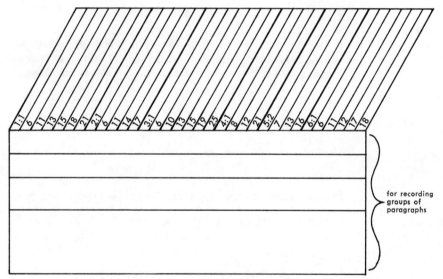

for recording groups of paragraphs

First, mark in your Bible the paragraph divisions as shown on Chart D. It is very important to be paragraph-conscious as you study the Bible text. The best way to mark the divisions in your Bible is to draw a horizontal line at the beginning of each paragraph, to the very edge of the page.

Now read each paragraph, picking up a paragraph title as you read. Do not do this exercise too slowly. Remember, detailed analysis comes later. Record your paragraph titles on Chart D.

IV. IDENTIFYING GROUPS OF PARAGRAPHS AND CHAPTERS.

Now read your entire group of paragraph titles. Could any of these be grouped together under a common subject? You may or may not see any groupings from your paragraph titles. Don't hesitate to glance back at the Bible text for clues to groups. Record any findings in the horizontal spaces shown at the bottom of Chart D.

Think next in terms of chapters. Do you see any ways to group chapters according to common subject?

What part of the epistle is mostly practical?

What part is mostly doctrinal?

What part is mostly autobiographical?

V. OBSERVING KEY WORDS AND KEY VERSES.

1. By now you have recognized many words of Galatians which have been repeated often throughout the letter. Make a list of these. (Sometimes a phrase is involved.)

_____

_____

_____

_____

2. Also, some verses have no doubt stood out as very

prominent in the book. What are these? _____

_____

_____

3. You may be ready at this point to identify a main theme of Galatians. What basically is Paul's main burden in writing this letter? State this in your own words. _____

_____

_____

Let one of the key verses which you have chosen be a key verse for the book, if it represents this main theme.

GALATIANS SET FREE FROM BONDAGE

"Magna Charta of spiritual emancipation" Favorite epistle of the Reformers.

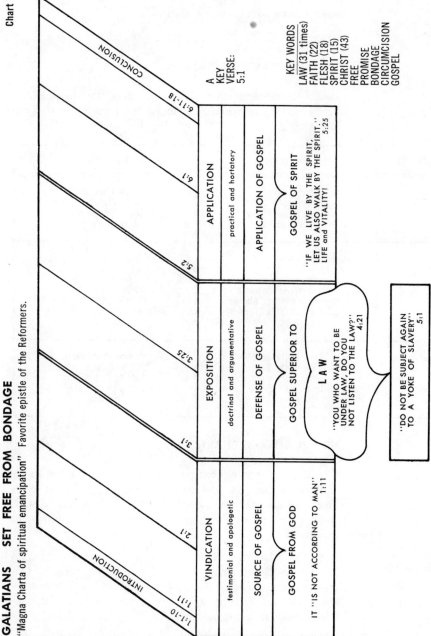

INTRODUCTION 1:1-10	VINDICATION 1:11		EXPOSITION 3:1		APPLICATION 5:2		CONCLUSION 6:11-18
	testimonial and apologetic		doctrinal and argumentative		practical and hortatory		
	SOURCE OF GOSPEL		DEFENSE OF GOSPEL		APPLICATION OF GOSPEL		
	GOSPEL FROM GOD		GOSPEL SUPERIOR TO		GOSPEL OF SPIRIT		
	IT "IS NOT ACCORDING TO MAN" 1:11		L A W "YOU WHO WANT TO BE UNDER LAW, DO YOU NOT LISTEN TO THE LAW?" 4:21		"IF WE LIVE BY THE SPIRIT, LET US ALSO WALK BY THE SPIRIT." 5:25 LIFE and VITALITY!		

"DO NOT BE SUBJECT AGAIN TO A YOKE OF SLAVERY" 5:1

A KEY VERSE: 5:1

KEY WORDS
LAW (31 times)
FAITH (22)
FLESH (18)
SPIRIT (15)
CHRIST (43)
FREE
PROMISE
BONDAGE
CIRCUMCISION
GOSPEL

19

4. Try assigning a short title to the letter, in line with the main theme which you have identified. _____

VI. CONTRASTS IN GALATIANS.

Galatians is clearly a book of contrasts. Try to recall as many of these as you can. Then compare your list with the following:[2]

CHAPTER	The Lower	The Higher
1—2	lost in Adam all die physically in Adam another gospel (false) man's reasoning	saved in Christ all live spiritually in Christ the genuine gospel God's revelation
3—4	law works curse of death condemnation by works servants in bondage (defeat) old covenant (symbolized by Hagar)	grace faith blessing of life justification by faith sons in freedom (victory) new covenant (symbolized by Sarah)
5—6	living in the flesh works of the flesh falling from grace world or self the object of glorying	walking in the Spirit fruit of the Spirit standing firm in grace the cross the sole object of glorying

VII. A SURVEY CHART.

Chart E is a survey chart of Galatians, showing the kinds of things which you have been looking for in the exercises above. Study this chart and compare its observations with those which you have made. Add studies of your own to the chart.

Note the following on Chart E:
1. The epistle is clearly divided into three parts of two chapters each. Observe that the practical section follows the doctrinal. Paul always bases his applications on doctrinal truths firmly established.

[2] List is adapted from Merrill F. Unger, *Unger's Bible Handbook*, p. 659.

2. A new division is made at 5:2 in order to show 5:1, with its theme of liberty, as a concluding verse to the previous section about liberty (e.g., note the word "free" in 4:26, 30-31).

3. The first ten verses of the letter are seen here as the introduction. Some versions and commentaries consider only 1:1-5 or 1:1-9 as the introduction. In our analysis of Lesson 3 we will study more closely the functions of the paragraph 1:6-10.

4. The conclusion of the epistle is identified as 6:11-18. If it were not for verse 11, can you see why only 6:17-18 might be considered as the conclusion?

5. The title "Set Free from Bondage" reflects the key verse 5:1, with its reference to a "yoke of bondage." What is the practical command of 5:1?

VIII. THE SUBJECT OF LAW IN GALATIANS.

In your analytical studies of the lessons that follow, a subject which will engage much of your time will be that of God's law and its relation to the Christian today. More will be said about this in the lessons that follow, but it will be helpful for you at this time to have clear in your mind what Paul is saying and does not say about the law in his epistle. Study carefully Chart F and the observations made concerning it.

Observations

1. Salvation is always by faith, whatever the time period. (For example, Abraham was saved through faith, 3:9.)

2. The crucial event in the gospel of atonement is the crucifixion of Christ. All human history relates ultimately to Christ's death. Read 3:13 for the relationship of the cross to the law.

3. Compared with that of Old Testament saints, the spiritual life of a believer in New Testament times is more *personally* identified with God, because "Christ liveth in me" (2:20).

4. Paul does not write that the law was evil or that it did

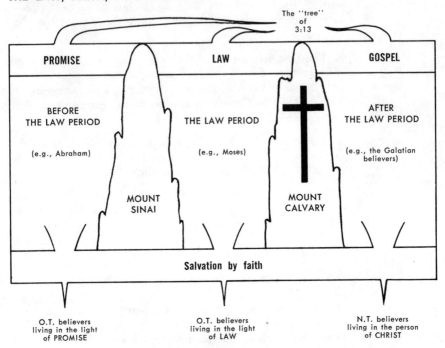

not fulfill its purposes (e.g., 3:24). It was fulfilled in Christ, who brought in a new dispensation or era (cf. 4:3-5).

IX.   A CONCLUDING EXERCISE.

Here is a list of some key verses in Galatians. Read them in the light of the survey study of Galatians which you have now completed. Let them whet your appetite for the spiritual feasts of the Bible texts which are to be analyzed in the lessons that follow.

Jot down practical lessons taught by these verses:

1:15-16 _____

_____

2:16 _____

2:20 _____

_____

3:3 _____

_____

3:8 _____

_____

3:13 _____

_____

4:4-6 _____

_____

5:1 _____

_____

5:14 _____

_____

5:22-23 _____

_____

5:25 _____

_____

6:2, 5 _____

_____

6:14 _____

_____

Paul's Introduction
to His Epistle

A GOOD INTRODUCTION OF A BOOK

TELLS AT LEAST IN A GENERAL

WAY WHAT THE BOOK IS ALL ABOUT.

The opening verses of Galatians serve this function well. After a salutation (1:1-2) and benediction (1:3-5), Paul reveals the trouble in the Galatian churches which caused him to write the letter (1:6-10). From what he says in these verses we may expect to find in the letter an exposé of a perversion of the true gospel.

We are living in a day when the gospel message is often twisted and falsely represented by those who claim to be servants of Christ. The passage of this lesson shows by Paul's example how we should react to this kind of subversion. The epistle is that contemporary.

I. PREPARATION FOR STUDY.

1. Have pencil (or pen) and paper handy at all times to record observations, interpretations and applications in the course of your study.

2. Whenever you read the Bible text, make notations on the pages of your Bible concerning things which strike you. Especially underline key words and phrases, and show connections between these by the use of lines.

3. Read the salutations of other epistles of Paul (e.g., 1 Corinthians and Ephesians), observing some of his favorite phrases for such opening greetings. Compare the length of these with that of Galatians' salutation.

II. ANALYSIS.

Segment to be analyzed[1]: 1:1-10.
Paragraph divisions: at verses 1 and 6.

A. The Segment as a Whole.

1. Read the segment and identify the content of each of these three parts:

1:1-2 _____

_____

1:3-5 _____

_____

1:6-10 _____

_____

2. Compare the tones of 1:1-5 and 1:6-10. _____

_____

_____

Account for the difference. _____

_____

_____

3. In what way does this segment serve as an introduction

to the epistle? _____

_____

_____

B. Paragraph by Paragraph.
1. SALUTATION AND BENEDICTION: 1:1-5.
Study carefully each word of the salutation of verses 1 and

2. See how many truths you can find here. Record these on paper.

---

[1] The word *segment* in these self-study guides means a unit of study which is a group of paragraphs. It may be the length of a chapter, or longer, or shorter.

What words does Paul use to identify Christians, including

himself? _____

_____

Do any similar words appear in the second paragraph?

_____

_____

What significant truths are taught by each word? _____

_____

_____

Paul was not one of the original twelve apostles. In what
sense, then, could he call himself an apostle (1:1)? (Cf.
1 Co 15:7.) What did Paul want to establish at the very
moment he wrote the word "apostle"? (See the parenthesis
of v. 1.) Observe that the first word of the parenthesis is
the negative "not," an early indicator of the polemic
character of the epistle. What cardinal doctrine appears in

this parenthesis? _____

_____

Compare the beginning and ending of the benediction:
  grace and peace to you (1:3)
  glory to him (1:5).
Why is the biblical order always "grace and peace," and

not "peace and grace"? _____

_____

Is it true that an underlying want of the unregenerate heart

is peace? _____

_____

Relate this to the comment that "grace remits sin, and
peace quiets the conscience." Ponder also these words:
"Left to himself, man is at odds with himself and the

world. He knows this whenever he begins to think seriously about himself and is not content to live like a cabbage."[2] How does verse 3 teach that Jesus is God? _____

_____

_____

Why is this a basic Christian doctrine? _____

_____

What cardinal doctrine appears in the middle of this benediction (v. 4)? _____

_____

_____

Relate this to the one observed in verse 1. _____

_____

_____

Analyze the two aspects of Christ's work referred to in verse 4. A breakdown of the phrases would look something like this:

gave	Himself	for our sins
deliver	us	from this present evil world

What does Paul mean by the last phrase, "deliver us from this present evil world"? _____

_____

_____

2. OCCASION OF THE LETTER: 1:6-10.
Underline in your Bible the various words that refer to the trouble in the Galatian churches. Why does Paul use such

[2] William Neil, *The Letter of Paul to the Galatians*, p. 92.

strong language? _____

_____

_____

Compare Paul's attitudes (1) in correcting the Galatian believers (v. 6), and (2) in exposing the evils of the intruders (e.g., v. 9). Concerning the former, is Paul following the rule which he lays down in 6:1? Explain.

_____

Observe in the progression of the paragraph how Paul moves from the subject of preaching by troublemakers (vv. 6-7) to that of his own preaching (v. 10).
Read verse 6. Analyze the defection:

"removed from _____

unto _____ "

Who is referred to by "him"? _____
Is there anything more wonderful than the "grace of Christ"? Does this account for the first two words of the

sentence, "I marvel"? _____
Read verse 7. The phrase "which is not another" refers back to "another gospel" of verse 6. Actually, two different Greek words are translated in the King James Version by the one word "another." A literal translation would read something like this:
   ". . . unto a *different* gospel:" (v. 6)
   "which is not [just] *another of the same kind*" (v. 7)
Study the entire verse 7 with these translations in mind. Were the troublemakers preaching the true gospel with only minor variations? How is this question answered by Paul's use of the words "pervert" (v. 7) and "accursed"

(vv. 8-9)? _____

_____

This idea of "another gospel" appears again in verses 8 and 9 in the phrase "any other." Some versions translate the original text here as "contrary," which strengthens the description "different" of verse 6. Compare verses 8 and 9. Is there any significant difference between the verses? Why the repetition? _____

Read verse 10. (Translate "persuade" as "seek to win over.") What was Paul's motivation in preaching the gospel? _____

How does he bring in the word "servant" in this context? _____

Does Paul's "anathema" of verse 8 and 9 reveal him to be an easygoing men-pleaser? _____

Does Galatians 1:10 contradict what Paul later wrote in 1 Corinthians 10:33 about pleasing men? _____

According to the Corinthian passage, what was a prime motive in his ministry to people? _____

III. NOTES.

1. "Ye are so soon removed" (1:6). The Greek tense calls for a *continuation* aspect in the translation. One good translation is the Berkeley: "You are so readily *turning away*."

2. "Accursed" (1:8-9). Read Isaiah 34:5; Zechariah 14:11; and Malachi 4:6 for the Hebrew counterpart of this Greek word *anathema*. The other times Paul uses the word in the New Testament are in these places: Romans 9:3; 1 Corinthians 12:3; 16:22.

IV. FOR THOUGHT AND DISCUSSION.

1. Why are the doctrines of Christ's death (1:4) and resurrection (1:1) foundational in the Christian faith?

29

2. "The church is a tender plant. It must be watched." These were Martin Luther's reflections as he read the text, "I marvel that ye are so soon removed." In what ways are churches today endangered by the same kind of false teachers which troubled the Galatian churches? How do you explain why a local church today, having received the Word of God as zealously as the Galatians, will so quickly let go of it? What can be done to help guard the witness of a local church?

3. Make a list of twenty strong words appearing in this passage. What thoughts come to you as you ponder each word in isolation? If you are studying in a group, discuss these. The following words are examples: dead, grace, sins, deliver, glory, evil world, will of God, gospel.

V. FURTHER STUDY.

1. Make extended studies of these words: apostle, servant, brethren, church. You are interested here in learning (1) the root meaning of the word; (2) how the word is used in the Bible. For help in such study, there are two basic aids:
  an exhaustive concordance of the Bible[3]
  a book on word studies[4]

2. Begin working on a character study of Paul in Galatians, keeping in mind that these are the early years of Paul's evangelistic ministry. Add to this project as you complete each succeeding lesson.

VI. WORDS TO PONDER.

There are some people who are upsetting you and trying to change the gospel of Christ. (1:7b, TEV).

---

[3] Two standard works are: James Strong, *The Exhaustive Concordance of the Bible*; and Robert Young, *Analytical Concordance to the Bible*.
[4] A recommended book is W. E. Vine, *An Expository Dictionary of New Testament Words*.

Source of Paul's Gospel

PAUL NOW TURNS TO A DEFENSE OF

HIS PREACHING, INSISTING ITS

SOURCE IS NONE OTHER THAN GOD.

As far as he is concerned, the gospel preached by him is infinitely greater than himself. He is not urging the Galatians to accept *him*, really. His sole passion is that they continue to embrace the message sent from God, to keep on living in the faith which it exalts, and thus to share this message with others still outside the family of God.

The first two chapters of Galatians are mostly *testimonial*. As you read the passage of this lesson it will encourage and inspire you to learn how plain and unsophisticated were the religious experiences of this man of God who authored such masterpieces of doctrine in the New Testament.

I. PREPARATION FOR STUDY.

1. Read the preceding passage (1:1-10) as a review, and note that Paul has been defending these three things:
a) the divine source of his apostleship (what verse?)
b) the gospel which he preached (does he cite the specifics of this gospel?)
c) his motives in preaching (what verse?)
Now, in the passage of this lesson, he will clearly verify that the gospel which he was preaching had its source in God, not in himself, or in other people, or in organizations.

2. Chart G shows the general contents of chapters 1 and 2. Keep this context in mind as you study these chapters.

3. Review Chart A for the geography of this passage. Three regions and four cities are prominent in the setting. Visualize this geography as you study the lesson. The relationships of the places are shown in this diagram:

31

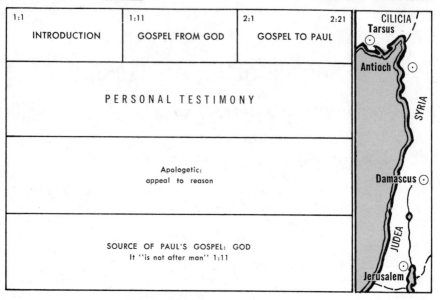

II.   ANALYSIS.

Segment to be analyzed: 1:11-24.
Paragraph divisions: at verses 11, 13, 15, 18, 21.

A.   The Segment as a Whole.

1. After you have marked the paragraph divisions in your
Bible, read the entire segment as one unit. What are your

initial impressions? _____

_____

_____

_____

2. In what paragraphs does Paul cite specific events in his

religious experience? _____
In what way does the first paragraph (1:11-12) serve to

introduce the theme of the passage? _____

_____

What is that theme? _____

_____

3. In what paragraphs does Paul emphasize the absence of any extended consultation with, or instruction by, other

leaders of the church? _____

_____

What is Paul's reason for doing this? _____

4. Note references to *time* in the segment. Study carefully Chart H, which shows a chronological sequence of Paul's experiences before and after his conversion. How long was Paul's stay in Arabia and Damascus? About how long did he minister in Syria and Cilicia between the first

THE CHRONOLOGY OF 1:11—2:1

Chart H

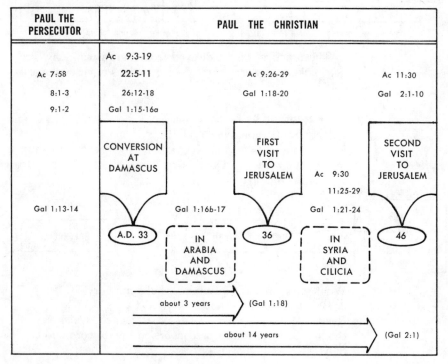

33

and second visits to Jerusalem? _____

_____

The following comments refer to the chronology of Chart
H:

1. There are problems in connection with any attempt to
harmonize the two accounts of Acts and Galatians. One
of the major points of difference is whether the second
visit to Jerusalem (Gal 2:1) was at the time of the famine
(Ac 11:27-30) or the Jerusalem council (Ac 15). (See
Further Study.)

2. The references "three years" and "fourteen years" probably do not mean strictly three and fourteen *twelve-month
periods*, respectively. In such references the Bible follows
what is common everyday usage by man. For example, the
"fourteen years" of Galatians 2:1 could mean something
like this, involving only part of A.D. 33 and of A.D. 46:

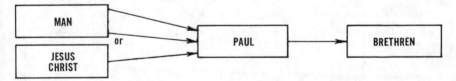

A.D.	33	34	35	36	37	38	39	40	41	42	43	44	45	46
	1	2	3	4	5	6	7	8	9	10	11	12	13	14

interval: twelve full years plus parts of two other calendar years

3. The practical truths derived from Paul's testimony are
not weakened by any unresolved questions of chronological
dates.

B. Paragraph by Paragraph.

1. SUBJECT INTRODUCED: 1:11-12.
Complete the following diagram to represent these two
introductory verses. Do this by associating a verb with
each of the four arrows.

MAN	
	or → PAUL → BRETHREN
JESUS CHRIST	

What does this suggest about Paul's ministry?

2. BEFORE PAUL'S CONVERSION: 1:13-14.
Read the following New Testament passages which reveal
the highlights of Paul's preconversion life. Record observations.

34

Ancestry and education

2 Co 11:22 _____

Ro 11:1 _____

Phil 3:4-5 _____

Ac 21:39 _____

22:3 _____

23:34 _____

23:6 _____

26:4 _____

Character
Phil 3:6 _____

1 Ti 1:12-13 _____

Persecutor
Ac 7:57-58 _____

8:1 _____

8:3-4 _____

22:4-5; 19-20 _____

26:9-11 _____

1 Co 15:9 _____

Now read Galatians 1:13-14. Observe that only a few lines
are devoted to Paul's preconversion years. This does not
mean that Paul thought lightly of the experiences of those
years. His purpose here is to give a brief biographical
résumé as *background* for the point he is about to establish
concerning the source of the gospel. What is Paul saying

in these verses, basically? _____

_____

_____

Observe the comparisons which Paul makes, introduced by
these words:
    "beyond" (v. 13)
    "above" (v. 14)
    "more exceedingly" (v. 14)

In what three ways does Paul refer to his Jewish associates before conversion? _____

_____

_____

Note the phrase, "I persecuted the church of God" (v. 13). Do you think Paul regarded Christians as "church of

TEXTUAL RE-CREATION OF GALATIANS 1:15-17   Chart I

BIBLE TEXT		
Main Statement	Description and Amplification	Outline
"But when it pleased God,		
	who SEPARATED me from my mother's womb,	SOVEREIGN ELECTION
	and CALLED me by his grace,	DIVINE CALLING
to reveal his Son in me,		NEW BIRTH
	that I might PREACH him among the heathen;	APOSTOLIC COMMISSION
immediately I CONFERRED NOT WITH FLESH AND BLOOD:		INDEPENDENCE (no consultation with man)
	neither went I up to Jerusalem to them which were apostles before me;	
	but I went into Arabia, and [then] returned again unto Damascus."	SOLITUDE (communion with God)

God" while he was persecuting them? _____

Read "profited" (v. 14) as "was advancing." (Compare the reading of v. 14 in a contemporary version.) Read Philippians 3:4-6, which gives a similar testimony of Paul.

3. CONVERSION AND EARLY YEARS AS A CHRISTIAN: 1:15-17.

Read Acts 9:3-25 for the account of Paul's conversion and early witnessing for Christ. You will note that Luke's account in Acts does not make any reference to a visit to Arabia (Gal 1:17). The visit to Arabia probably took place between Acts 9:22 and 9:23.[1]

The textual re-creation of this paragraph (Chart I) analyzes the Bible text phrase by phrase. Study this exercise very carefully so that you will be able to make your own textual re-creation of other passages in Galatians. This step in analytical study is a key to a full understanding of what the Bible author is saying. It is especially valuable in analyzing a long sentence. (Note that your King James Version translates the entire paragraph as one long sentence.) Observe the following in this textual re-creation:

a) The main statement, shown in the left-hand vertical column, is the basic assertion of the text. The CORE (main subject, main verb, main object) is the statement,

"I" (main subject)

"CONFERRED NOT" (main verb)

"WITH FLESH AND BLOOD" (main object)

This core shows us the *main* point which Paul is getting across among the many things he wants to say. Actually, the core is bolstered by the last two points in column 2, including the interesting reference to Arabia.

b) Study the outline shown in the right-hand column. Observe especially in the first half of the paragraph how much Paul has compacted into his testimony. As a writer, he was a master of precise and concise theological terminology.

If Paul's main point here is that he did not derive his message from *human* sources, does he say in these verses where that message came from? _____

---

[1] See Frank J. Goodwin, *A Harmony of the Life of St. Paul*, p. 26.

What contrast is suggested by the words "Jerusalem" and "Arabia"? (See *Notes* on Arabia.) _____

_____

If the place in Arabia to which Paul went was Mount Sinai (cf. 4:25), what contribution would the symbolism of geography have made to Paul's experience? _____

_____

In view of the context, what does the word "but" in 1:17*b* suggest about the *kind* of experience which was Paul's in Arabia? _____

_____

Why do you think Scripture is silent about such specifics?

_____

_____

Note the reference to three years in verse 18. Can you tell from the context how much of those three years was spent in Arabia (v. 17), and how much in Damascus after re-turning from Arabia (v. 17)? _____

_____

4. VISITS WITH PETER AND JAMES: 1:18-20.
Review Chart H for the occasion of this first visit of Paul to Jerusalem after his conversion. Read Acts 9:26-29 for Luke's account of this visit. The reference to "apostles" in verse 27 could be called a "generalizing plural," for in Galatians 1:18-19 Paul says he saw only Peter and James of the apostles.[2] Of Paul's two visits (to Peter, and to James) at this time, which seems to have been the main one, according to Galatians 1:18-19? _____

_____

As of Acts 9, when Paul visited Peter, Peter had not yet experienced the important vision convincing him that the gospel was for Gentiles as well as for Jews (Ac 10). How did the fact of such a conference at that early date bolster Paul's point in Galatians that consultation with men was

_____

[2] Actually, this James was not one of the twelve apostles. Paul regarded him as one of the Jerusalem church's key leaders. (Cf. Ac 12:17; 15:13; 21:18; Gal 2:9.) Compare Ac 14:14 and 1 Co 15:5-7 for various uses of the word "apostle."

not the source of his message, namely, that salvation for Gentiles was through faith, not through faith *plus* becoming a Jew? _____

_____

The James which Paul saw at this time was probably the writer of the epistle of James. In view of this epistle's emphasis on works, how would the fact of a conference between these two apostles bolster Paul's point in Galatians?

5. MINISTRY IN SYRIA AND CILICIA: 1:21-24.
Review Chart H again for the setting of this paragraph. Then read the passages cited there, namely, Acts 9:30; 11:25-30. No details are given in the New Testament about Paul's ten years of ministering in Syria and Cilicia at this time (A.D. 36-46). It is interesting to observe that places like Tarsus, Paul's hometown, were not evangelized on any of Paul's three missionary journeys (A.D. 47-56). This may be because of the decade of ministry reported in Galatians 1:21-24. The Acts 15:41 passage about "confirming the churches" of Syria and Cilicia on Paul's second journey is seen by some to refer at least partly to churches earlier evangelized during the years of Galatians 1:21.

Galatians 1:21 is about what provinces? _____

_____

The remaining verses of the paragraph are about what province? _____

_____

Since Paul has just written about Jerusalem, a city of Judea, in the previous paragraph, he must be referring in verse 22 to churches of Judea outside of Jerusalem. (Cf. Ac 9:31 with Gal 1:24.)
As of this time in Paul's Christian experience, did the Judean churches feel that Paul was preaching a distorted gospel? Base your answer on 1:22-24. _____

_____

What do you consider to be the key phrases of this paragraph? Explain why. _____

_____

_____

_____

_____

What is Paul's main point in this paragraph? _____

_____

What does it contribute to what he has already estab-

lished? _____

III. NOTES.

1. "Separate me from my mother's womb" (1:15). Read Jeremiah 1:5 for a similar reference to predestination.

2. "Immediately I conferred not" (1:16). This is a reference to an avoidance of instruction from other Christians (called "flesh and blood" here to contrast *human* instruction with the *divine* revelation of v. 16a). The question is raised as to whether this "immediately" of Galatians contradicts the "straightway" of Acts 9:20 (read the verse). Of this, Frank Goodwin comments, "Luke evidently uses 'straightway' (Acts 9:20) in a strictly literal sense. . . . In Galatians Paul's use of historical facts is all subservient to his argument, which is to assert his dependence upon God alone for the gospel he preached. . . . It is natural that his 'immediately' should be used, in such a hasty sketch, in a free, general sense as meaning *soon after* his conversion, which can allow time for the preaching in the synagogues mentioned in Ac 9:20."[3]

3. "Arabia" (1:17). This is a loose geographical term as used in Paul's day. Then it referred to areas as far south as the Sinai Peninsula and as far north as the Syrian Desert. Many Bible students hold that Paul's stay in Arabia was in a desert area near Damascus. Those who hold that it may have been at Mount Sinai take the suggestion from Galatians 4:25 ("mount Sinai in Arabia"), and liken such an experience to that of Moses and Elijah there.

4. "Was unknown by face" (1:22). A paraphrase of this phrase might read like this: "remained unknown personally."

[3] Goodwin, p. 203.

IV. FOR THOUGHT AND DISCUSSION.

1. The conversion of Paul has been called by one writer "the death of the man he had been, and the birth of the man he had become."[4] What is involved in the new birth of a sinner ("born again," Jn 3:7)? Think of such things as the working of God, the conditions to be fulfilled in the sinner's heart, and the fruits of such a regeneration.

2. When Paul was saved, he surely didn't anticipate all the various kinds of opposition which he would encounter from within the fellowship of believers. What do you think was his main reason for not seeking instruction from leaders in the church in those first years? Do you think that God may have given him clear directions concerning this?

3. How do you think Paul occupied himself during his stay in Arabia, which was probably spent in solitude? How much knowledge did he already have of (1) Old Testament Scripture, (2) the church's use of the Old Testament, (3) reports about the life and ministry of Christ?

In view of his spiritual background up to the time of his conversion, what were his spiritual needs now that he was a saved man? What were his needs in view of the ministry ahead of him? (See Ac 9:15-16.)

V. FURTHER STUDY.

1. Consult various commentaries for the harmonizing of the chronology of Paul's experiences after his conversion as recorded in Acts and Galatians. Study especially the question as to whether the trip to Jerusalem recorded in Galatians 2:1 was the famine visit (Ac 11:27-30) or the Jerusalem council (Ac 15).

2. If you have not made an extended study of the subject of *apostles* (Lesson 3), you may want to do so now. Include in your study such verses as Acts 1:22; 10:41; 1 Corinthians 9:1; 15:5-9.

VI. WORDS TO PONDER.

They gave glory to God because of me (1:24, Living Bible).

---

[4] William Neil, *The Letter of Paul to the Galatians*, p. 28.

Confirmation
by Jerusalem Leaders

PAUL HAS MORE TO WRITE ABOUT

THE GOSPEL MESSAGE WHICH HE HAS

BEEN PREACHING TO THE GENTILES.

In chapter 1 he emphasized that his message was by revelation from God, and not by instruction from man. Now he will show that his mission to the Gentiles (of which the Galatian churches were a part) was wholeheartedly endorsed by the Jewish leaders of the Jerusalem church. So Paul was claiming (1) *divine revelation of the message*, and (2) *human endorsement of the mission.*

I. PREPARATION FOR STUDY.

1. When read in connection with the Acts account, the reference of Galatians 2:1 to a fourteen-year interval reminds us that during most of that time the apostle was on his own, working independently of other leaders of the early church. From a human standpoint, he "had had to work out his own interpretation of the gospel in the light of his conversion experience and such guidance as he had received from other missionaries in his early days as a Christian."[1] Imagine you were Paul during those years. You were well aware that as of then most Christians, including the leaders of the church, were Jewish Christians. But God had sent you with the gospel primarily to Gentiles (Ac 9:15). What thoughts would be going through your mind as to how you might reach these people and convince them that the message of Christ was for Gentile as well as Jew?

2. Review Chart H, which shows the visit to Jerusalem of Galatians 2:1 as Paul's *second* visit, in A.D. 46. Chart J is an excerpt of Chart H.

---

[1] William Neil, *The Letter of Paul to the Galatians*, p. 35.

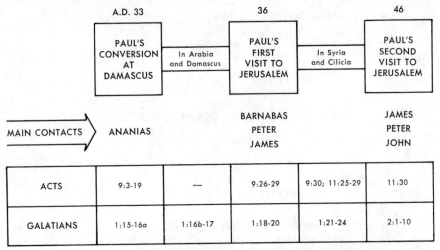

	A.D. 33		36		46
	PAUL'S CONVERSION AT DAMASCUS	In Arabia and Damascus	PAUL'S FIRST VISIT TO JERUSALEM	In Syria and Cilicia	PAUL'S SECOND VISIT TO JERUSALEM
MAIN CONTACTS	ANANIAS		BARNABAS PETER JAMES		JAMES PETER JOHN
ACTS	9:3-19	—	9:26-29	9:30; 11:25-29	11:30
GALATIANS	1:15-16a	1:16b-17	1:18-20	1:21-24	2:1-10

As noted earlier, this manual is following the view that Galatians 2:1 and Acts 11:30 (famine visit) report the same visit.[2] Where has Paul been ministering during the period between the first and second visits? _____

_____

3. The experience of Peter recorded in Acts 10:1—11:18 (read this passage) took place while Paul was ministering in Syria and Cilicia, *after* his visit to Peter (Gal 1:18). Do you think it was long before Paul heard about Peter's experience? What would such a report do for Paul, engaged as he was in a ministry to Gentiles? _____

_____

4. Now read Acts 11:19-30 for more specific background to the famine visit noted above. After you have read the passage, answer the following:
a) What was the occasion for the first evangelization of the city of Antioch (Ac 11:19-21)? _____

_____

---

[2] Keep in mind that an effective study of Gal 2:1-10 is not jeopardized by the open question as to whether Gal 2:1 ff. is to be identified with the famine visit (Ac 11:30) or the Jerusalem conference (Ac 15).

b) Why did the church of Jerusalem send Barnabas to Antioch (Ac 11:22-24)? _____

_____

c) Why do you think Barnabas brought Paul to Antioch (Cf. Ac 11:25-26)? _____

_____

d) Compare Acts 11:22 and 11:30. What part does Barnabas play in each verse? _____

_____

II. ANALYSIS.

Segment to be analyzed: 2:1-10.
Paragraph divisions: at verses 1, 6.

A. The Segment as a Whole.

1. Read the passage through once, for general impressions. Record some of these. Do you recall reading any reference to the delivery of a famine offering sent by the Antioch church? Verse 10 only makes a general reference to the needs of the poor, though its appearance here may be more than coincidental. On this, Neil comments: "The only direct request of the Church leaders was that Paul and Barnabas should bear in mind the hardships of the relatively poor Jerusalem church, which was precisely what had brought them to Jerusalem in the first place!"[3] This kind of omission in reporting was repeated later, when the delivery of Paul's offering to the Jerusalem poor (1 Co 16:1-4) was not reported by Luke in Acts 21:15 ff. How can you account for such omissions? Does this tell you anything about *priorities* in the Christian ministry? What main point is Paul trying to establish in Galatians 2:1-10 concerning this visit to Jerusalem? _____

_____

2. Try reading the segment in this manner: Read each verse *alternately* in your King James version and in a modern version. (There are some verses in this passage which are awkwardly translated in the King James.)

[3] Neil, p. 37.

3. In what kind of tone does Paul write here? _____

_____

B. Paragraph by Paragraph.

1. PAUL STATES HIS CASE: 2:1-5.
This is Paul's story of the part *he* played in this important visit to the Jerusalem church, fourteen years after his conversion.[4] (In Luke's account of Ac 11:30, *Barnabas* was apparently the leader of the party as far as the famine offering project was concerned. Note the order: "Barnabas and Saul.") Whom did Paul invite along with him? _____

_____

How much do you know about this companion from these

verses? (See *Notes.*) _____

_____

The famine visit was commissioned by the Antioch church (Ac 11:29-30). What was Paul's special mission to be accomplished on that same journey, according to Galatians

2:2? _____
What does Paul mean by the words, "I went up by revela-

tion" (2:2)? _____

_____

With whom, specifically, did Paul have this conference?

_____

Compare the phrases, "were of reputation" (v. 2); "seemed to be somewhat" (v. 6); "seemed to be pillars" (v. 9).
What did Paul want to hear from the Jerusalem leaders

(2:2)? (Refer to a modern version reading of 2:2.) _____

_____

How was Titus a test case on this occasion? _____

_____

Who wanted to have him circumcised? _____

_____

[4] The phrase "Then fourteen years after" could be paraphrased, "Next, fourteen years later."

(See *Notes* on the word *circumcised.*) Who refused to give in to such a demand? _____

_____

On what grounds was the refusal made? _____

_____

Do you think God had anything to do with Paul's inviting Titus along on the trip? _____

What are the two key contrasting words of 2:4? _____

_____

According to 2:5*b*, what was at stake in this Titus test case? _____

_____

If Paul had not yet evangelized these Galatian churches as of the time of this Jerusalem visit, what did he mean by the phrase "might continue with you" (2:5*b*)? _____

_____

2. THE CHURCH LEADERS GIVE THEIR SUPPORT: 2:6-10. What is the key repeated pronoun of this paragraph? What were the prominent pronouns of the first paragraph? _____

_____

Study this paragraph with these translations in mind:
a) Read "God accepteth no man's person" (v. 6) as "God shows no partiality" (NASB).
b) Read "added nothing to me" (v. 6) as "made no new suggestions to me" (TEV).
c) Read "gospel of the uncircumcision" (v. 7) as "gospel to the uncircumcised"; and "gospel of the circumcision" as "gospel to the circumcised" (NASB). Who are the circumcised, and who are the uncircumcised? _____

_____

d) Read "heathen" (v. 9) as "Gentiles." (The same Greek word is translated "Gentiles" in v. 8.)
What two things did the Jerusalem leaders recognize had

been given to Paul (2:7, 9)? (Cf. 1 Co 15:9-10; Eph 3:2.)

Is this paragraph about two messages, or two missions?

What was different about Peter's apostleship and Paul's apostleship? _____

What was symbolized by the "right hands of fellowship" (2:9)? _____
Whom did Paul recognize here to be "pillars" of the Jerusalem church (2:9)? _____

Do you take the parenthetical words of verse 6 as sarcastic? What did he mean by these words? _____
What was the significance of the request of verse 10, directed as it was to Gentiles who did not have the *national* heritage of the Jewish law? _____

III. NOTES.

1. "Took Titus with me" (2:1). Chronologically speaking, this is the earliest appearance of Titus in the New Testament. He is not part of the Acts story. Titus was probably converted through the ministry of Paul (cf. Titus 1:4), and became one of Paul's helpers.

2. "Circumcised" (2:3). The Judaizers disturbing the new Galatian Gentile Christians were saying that a Gentile must fulfill Jewish rites to be saved, in addition to believing. Circumcision, a symbolic seal of God's covenant with Israel (Gen 17:10-14), was one of those rites. When Paul referred to it in this setting, he meant all the Jewish rites and traditions which it represented.

3. "But neither Titus . . . was compelled to be circumcised" (2:3). The sentence structure of verses 3-5 is ad-

mitted by all to be very ambiguous. Some have read the verses as saying that Paul consented to circumcising Titus, but not by compulsion.[5] Most expositors take the other view.

4. "That the truth of the gospel might continue with you" (2:5). Even though Paul had not yet met his Galatian readers at the time of this conference with the Jerusalem leaders, when he wrote the epistle he viewed that former stand at Jerusalem, with the leaders, as prospectively assuring that the true gospel would continue to penetrate the uttermost parts of the world.

5. "James, Cephas, and John" (2:9). This James was the Lord's brother, writer of the epistle bearing his name. Cephas was Peter, writer of two New Testament epistles. John was the son of Zebedee, one of the twelve disciples (Mk 3:13-19), author of one of the four gospels, plus three epistles, and Revelation.

IV. FOR THOUGHT AND DISCUSSION.

What practical truths do you learn from this passage about the following:

1. getting directions from God concerning things to do and things to say (and not to say)

2. the liberty which Christians have in Christ Jesus; the possibilities of being ignorant of this blessing, of ignoring it, and of abusing it

3. the importance of contending earnestly for the faith once and for all delivered to God's people (cf. Jude 3)

4. the sense in which it is true that God has no favorites (2:6)

5. the need for Christian workers to recognize that although the gospel message is fixed, there are diversities of methods and spheres in the worldwide mission of evangelization.

6. the need for Christians to work in a spirit of unity, joining "right hands of fellowship"

7. the responsibility of Christians to help the poor in their times of need

[5] See Alexander Ross, "The Epistle to the Galatians" in, *The New Bible Commentary*, p. 1005.

V. FURTHER STUDY.

1. Study the usages of the words "reveal" and "revelation" in the New Testament.

2. Study the subject of "circumcision" in the Bible. Begin with the first appearance of the rite in Scripture, at Genesis 17:10-14. Consult a Bible dictionary for help.[6]

3. Make a character study of Titus in the New Testament. A concordance and a Bible dictionary should be consulted.

4. If you have not done so in a previous lesson, consult various commentaries on the question of when the visit of Galatians 2:1 took place.

VI. WORDS TO PONDER.

> We did not give those men [pseudo-Christians] an inch, for the truth of the gospel for you and all gentiles was at stake (2:5, Phillips).

---

[6] A good article appears in Merrill F. Unger, *Unger's Bible Dictionary*, pp. 206-7.

Confrontation with Peter

PAUL'S CONFRONTATION WITH PETER

PROBABLY TOOK PLACE SOON AFTER

PAUL HAD RETURNED TO ANTIOCH.

It was the third meeting of Paul and Peter, and not a pleasant one:

1. First meeting (at Jerusalem, A.D. 36): Paul becomes acquainted with Peter, and visits with him for fifteen days (Gal 1:18).

2. Second meeting (at Jerusalem, A.D. 46): Paul and Peter join "right hands of fellowship" in the ministry of the gospel, Paul as apostle to the Gentiles, and Peter as apostle to the Jews (Gal 2:1-10).

3. Third meeting (at Antioch, A.D. 46-47): Paul publicly

CONTEXT OF LESSON 6

Chart K

chapters 1-2			chapters 3-4		chapters 5-6	
TESTIMONIAL AND APOLOGETIC			DOCTRINAL AND ARGUMENTATIVE		PRACTICAL AND HORTATORY	
1:11 Sources of Paul's Gospel	2:1 Confirmation by Jerusalem Leaders	2:11 Confrontation with Peter				
4	5	6	7	8	9	10

INTRODUCTION / Lesson 3

rebukes Peter for being two-faced in his relations with Jewish and Gentile Christians.

The passage of this lesson is the concluding one in the two-chapter testimonial section of the epistle. See Chart K for its context. The blocked area is this lesson.

Paul was an honest minister of the gospel who did not hold back telling the truth even when it hurt. Actually, the fact of Paul's unpleasant encounter with Peter served to support his proof that he was not preaching the gospel under the thumb of anyone, including the apostles from Jerusalem. After you have completed your study of this lesson, you will appreciate why Paul was doubly disturbed over the problem about Jewish laws for Christians, when even a pillar of the church, like Peter, would compromise on the issue.

I. PREPARATION FOR STUDY.

1. One needs only to take a look at the New Testament record to sense how prominent the Jewish/Gentile-Christian problem was in the early ministry of Paul. This was the very problem to which the letter of Galatians was addressed, so it will be helpful now in our study to survey Paul's involvements as this thorny problem kept vexing the early Christian church. Chart L tabulates the five times the problem was dealt with. Study this chart and review passages which you have already analyzed in previous lessons. Record in the right-hand column what the problem was in each case. Was it always basically the same problem?

2. The name of James, brother of the Lord, appears in the passage of this lesson. At this time James was regarded as the head of the church in Jerusalem. (Read Ac 12:17; Gal 1:19; 2:9, 12.) Read Acts 21:18-26 for the part James played many years later in recommending that Paul join in a Nazarite vow for the sake of the thousands of Jewish Christians in Jerusalem. Note from this that the problem about a Gentile Christian's relation to the Mosaic law still lingered at the time of the close of Paul's third missionary journey.

3. Prepare a work sheet similar to Chart M, showing three blank paragraph boxes. Let this be the place where you record many of your observations in your analytical study.

PAUL'S INVOLVEMENTS IN THE FREQUENT APPEARANCES OF THE JEWISH-GENTILE PROBLEM

Chart L

DATE	EVENT	PASSAGE		SUBJECT DISCUSSED OR PROBLEM
A.D. 46	Second visit to Jerusalem	Ac 11:30 Gal 2:1-10	Lesson 5	SUBJECT: PROBLEM:
46	Return to Antioch Confrontation with Peter	Ac 12:25 Gal 2:11-21	this lesson	PROBLEM:
47	First missionary journey, to regions of Galatia	Ac 13—14		
47-48	Troublemakers move into the Galatian churches when Paul departs	(Gal 1:6-9; 3:1)		PROBLEM:
48	Return from first missionary journey	Ac 14:26-28		
48	Jewish-Christian legalists causing dissension in the Antioch church	Ac 15:1-2		PROBLEM:
49	Jerusalem council	Ac 15:3-29		PROBLEM:
49-52	Second missionary journey	Ac 15:36—18:22		

Feel free to record what *you* think is significant in the Bible text. Record words and phrases of the Bible text inside the boxes. Organize and record your own conclusions and outlines on a separate sheet of paper.

II. ANALYSIS.

Segment to be analyzed: 2:11-21.
Paragraph divisions: at verses 11, 14, 17.

A. The Segment as a Whole.

1. After you have marked the three paragraph divisions in your Bible, read the segment through for initial observations.

2. What key repeated words did you observe? _____

_____

3. What is the main content of each paragraph? Record on Chart M. (One such outline already appears on the chart.)

B. Paragraph by Paragraph.

1. THE PROBLEM SITUATION: 2:11-13.
Read 2:11-13. What group is Paul referring to by the phrase "them which were of the circumcision"? _____

_____

Read "dissembled" (v. 13) as "acted hypocritically," and "dissimulation" as "hypocrisy" (New Berkeley).
The issue of this paragraph concerned a Jewish tradition. In the case of Titus (2:3-5), it involved a Mosaic law of circumcision. Of the former, one writer has commented, "Although eating with Gentiles was not specifically forbidden by the Law of Moses, it had become traditional practice among orthodox Jews, in order to avoid any risk of eating 'unclean' food or of being contaminated by using utensils which had been in contact with it, that Jews and Gentiles should not sit down at the same table."[1] Would you say that in the circumcision and eating issues the same *principle* was involved? If so, what was that principle? _____

_____

Who went along with Peter's hypocrisy? What does this indicate as to how big a problem this issue still was?

_____

_____

2. PAUL REBUKES PETER: 2:14-16.
Read 2:14-16. Where do Paul's words to Peter begin? Is it clear in your Bible where they end? Compare various Bible versions to see the different views taken on this latter question. Whether or not verses 15-21 are the exact words of Paul to Peter (like v. 14), we may be certain

---

[1] William Neil, *The Letter of Paul to the Galatians*, p. 40.

main content

11

SITUATION

14

REBUKE

17

DOCTRINE

21

that at this time Paul shared with Peter their *content*.
Phillips' paraphrase represents 2:15a thus: "And then I
went on to explain that we, who are Jews. . . ."
According to 2:14a, what was Paul's sharp indictment of

Peter? _____

_____

_____

Why did Paul rebuke Peter publicly (2:14)? _____

_____

What would be the logical outcome of Peter's actions,

according to the last phrase of verse 14? _____

_____

How does Paul identify the true interpretation of the
gospel by a Jewish Christian like himself (2:15-16)?

_____

_____

Observe in these verses the three references to works and
the three references to faith. Record these on Chart L. Do
you think Peter agreed with this doctrine as stated by
Paul?
Evaluate this comment: "Whatever principle Peter thought
he was respecting was of no significance compared with the
gospel principle that he was violating."[2]
Note the repetition of the word *justified*. What does this

word mean? (See *Notes*.) How is a sinner justified? _____

_____

3. SALVATION: EITHER BY CHRIST, OR BY THE LAW: 2:17-21.
Paul now gets at the heart of the matter, as to why it is
false that the fulfilling of any Jewish law is a necessary
condition for salvation. This paragraph is a fitting conclusion to the biographical passages preceding it. Also, because it is solidly doctrinal, it is a transitional paragraph
introducing the doctrinal section (chaps. 3-4) which follows. Study this paragraph very carefully, phrase by
phrase and word by word. Record key words and phrases
on the analytical Chart M.

[2] Ibid., pp. 40-41.

King James	Expanded Paraphrase
2:17 But if, while we seek to be justified by Christ,	But we who are Jews by birth, since we seek our justification in Christ, as they [Gentiles] do, and not in the law,
we ourselves also are found sinners,	have been found out to be sinners as truly as those Gentiles.
is therefore Christ the minister of sin?	Does that mean, then, [when we talk about not keeping the law to be saved,] that Christ encourages sin?
God forbid.	No indeed! It is impossible on any pretext to go back to the old principle of justification by keeping the law.
2:18 For if I build again	If now I begin to rebuild
the things which I destroyed,	what I once pulled down,
I make myself a transgressor.	then indeed I do put myself in the position of a law-breaker; I confess that I was wrong in pointing to Christ rather than the law as the way of getting right with God.
2:19 But I through the law am dead to the law,	But it was the law itself that drove me to the point where I died in relation to it,
that I might live unto God.	so that I might enter upon a new life—a life lived for God.

Note the various references to Christ in this paragraph. Which of these refer to His death? (Note: The phrase "faith of Jesus Christ," v. 16, means "faith in Jesus Christ." Cf Ro 3:26.) _____

Note the references to the law. Is it correct to interpret that Paul is teaching this either-or truth: That if it is possible for a sinner to be saved by the law, then he is not saved by Christ? Support your answer with statements in the paragraph. _____

Read Psalm 143:2 for one example of the Old Testament scripture references which told Jews of Paul's day about those who were *not* justified. Observe in Psalm 143:1 a reference to God's righteousness, followed by the admission of 143:2 that "no man living is righteous before thee" (RSV).

The phrase "we ourselves also are found sinners" (2:17) is a reference to Jews, relating back to verse 15, "sinners of the Gentiles." Because it is difficult to grasp the full meaning of verses 17-19 in the King James translation, this translation is compared with a contemporary version on Chart N.[3] Study the two readings carefully.

Compare the following phrases, in their contexts:
"I . . . am dead" (2:19)
"I am crucified" (2:20)
"Christ is dead" (2:21)

Analyze verse 20 very carefully. This is one of the most precious (and oft-quoted) verses in the Bible. It is also one of the key passages of Galatians. Chart O shows some relationships between the main phrases of the verse.

a) Observe that Paul begins with a reference to Christ's death ("crucified with Christ") and ends by referring to the same key event ("gave himself for me").

b) Why is death of Christ such a vital doctrine in the Christian faith? _____

_____

_____

c) How is the law related to it? _____

---

[3]F. F. Bruce, *The Letters of Paul, An Expanded Paraphrase*, p. 25.

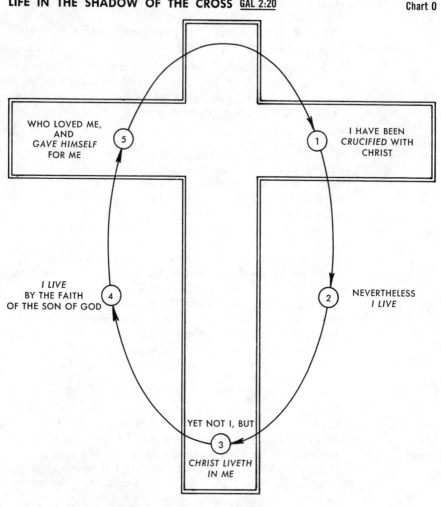

d) How does Paul bring this out in verse 21? _____

_____

e) Note: Chart O shows the first phrase of 2:20 as "I have been crucified," a correct translation as it appears in such versions as the New American Standard Bible. What does this perfect tense teach about a once-for-all experience

of a Christian? _____

_____

f) Compare Romans 6:6 with the first phrase of Galatians 2:20. _____

_____

g) Compare Romans 6:4-11 with the references of Galatians 2:20 to a believer's *living*. _____

_____

Observe the word "righteousness" in verse 21. Keep in mind that the Greek root of this word is the same as that of the word "justified" (vv. 15-17). How does this verse support verse 16? _____

_____

Note Paul's reference to "grace of God" (v. 21). How is it related to what Paul has just written in verse 20? _____

_____

III. NOTES.

1. "Antioch" (2:11). This, of course, is the Antioch of Syria, not the Antioch near Pisidia where Paul ministered on his first missionary journey. (See the map of Chart A.) Built in 301 B.C., it was the capital city of Syria. In Paul's day its population reached half a million. In the book of Acts the locations of the "headquarters" of the first-century program of evangelization were at these places, successively: Jerusalem, Antioch, Ephesus.

2. "Certain came from James" (2:12). At this time James was regarded as the head of the church at Jerusalem. "It is impossible to know in what relation these visitors stood to James and on precisely what mission they came."[4]

3. "He did eat with the Gentiles" (2:12). Jews avoided this kind of intimacy with Gentiles, but Peter was a Christian. As one writer has commented, Peter here recognized that "a Jewish Christian is a Christian first and a Jew second."

4. "He withdrew and separated himself" (2:12). This was

[4] Everett F. Harrison, "The Epistle to the Galatians," p. 1289.

Peter's sin, committed not with any malicious motive, but for the sake of expediency. However, Paul saw only compromise, hypocrisy and divisiveness in the act. For Paul, "this was a sheer betrayal of the gospel. It struck at the very roots of what it meant to be a Christian. Whatever principle Peter thought he was respecting was of no significance compared with the gospel principle that he was violating."[5]

5. "Sinners of the Gentiles" (2:15). In this verse the phrase is set over the phrase "Jews by nature," but it is not intended to imply that Jews are not sinners like the Gentiles (cf. v. 17). This is borne out by the continuation of thought here:

a) *"We* who are Jews" (v. 15)

b) "even *we* have believed" (v. 16)

c) "that *we* might be justified" (v. 16)

6. "Justified" (2:16). The Greek root of the word is "righteous." Justification is the opposite of condemnation (cf. Ro 8:33-34). Here is one definition of justification:

> Justification is an act of God's free grace, wherein He pardoneth all our sins, and accepteth us as righteous in His sight, only for the righteousness of Christ imputed to us, and received by faith alone.[6]

7. "I . . . am dead to the law" (2:19). Everett Harrison comments on this:

> The Law had done a service for Paul even if it had not brought him justification. Through the Law he had become dead to that very Law, for the Law had wrought a consciousness of sin which prepared him to accept Christ. It had also brought Christ to the cross in order to redeem those who had broken that Law. Christ was Paul's representative in that death to the Law.[7]

8. "Grace of God" (2:21). This is the "free, spontaneous, absolute loving-kindness of God toward men."[8] Can you add to this definition?

IV. FOR THOUGHT AND DISCUSSION.

1. Peter did not want to fellowship with Gentile Christians when the Jewish Christians from Jerusalem were

[5] Neil, pp. 40-41.
[6] *Westminster Shorter Catechism.*
[7] Harrison, p. 1290.
[8] Marvin R. Vincent, *Word Studies in the New Testament,* 4:109.

around. In effect, whom was he discriminating against? Are there any parallels in the Christian church today where Christians avoid other Christians for some reason or other? What are your thoughts about this?

2. Were Paul, Peter and Barnabas close friends on this occasion? In view of this, what good qualities do you see in Paul for taking a stand in rebuking these brethren?

3. What practical truths do you learn from each of the following phrases of 2:20:

a) "I am [have been] crucified with Christ."

b) "I live; yet not I, but Christ liveth in me."[9] (Study the *vine and branches* passage of Jn 15:1-8 in this connection.)

c) "I live *in* the faith which is *in* the Son of God" (free trans.)

d) "Who loved me, and gave himself for me."

4. Evaluate the following advice: "When the conscience is disturbed, do not seek advice from reason or from the Law, but rest your conscience in the grace of God and His Word, and proceed as if you had never heard of the Law."[10]

5. As a review exercise, go back over the Bible text of chapters 1 and 2, noting the various things Paul has written to convince his Galatian readers that the gospel which he preached to them was from God. Recall other important truths which he included in this *personal* section of his epistle.

V. FURTHER STUDY.

1. Study what the New Testament reveals about these two men: James (brother of the Lord), and Barnabas.

2. Try composing your own paraphrase of Galatians 2:14-21.[11]

VI. WORDS TO PONDER.

I am not one of those who treats Christ's death as meaningless (2:21a, Living Bible).

[9] Compare a modern version rendering of this text.
[10] Martin Luther, *A Commentary on St. Paul's Epistle to the Galatians;* p. 67.
[11] For an extensive paraphrase (43 lines) on the 14-line Bible text of Gal 2:14-21, see Vincent, pp. 109-10.

Faith and Law Compared

OUR STUDY NOW BEGINS THE SECOND

OF THE THREE MAJOR SECTIONS

OF GALATIANS, 3:1—5:1.

This middle section of the epistle is its doctrinal core, where Paul shines as a theologian instructed by God. The context of 3:1—5:1 is shown on Chart P, which reviews the overall structure of Galatians studied in Lesson 2.

We will be studying this doctrinal section (3:1—5:1) in two lessons. Our present lesson is about the subject *Faith and Law Compared*, as found in 3:1-24. In Lesson 8 the passage to be studied is 3:25—5:1, under the subject *Freedom in Christ*.

SURVEY OF GALATIANS   Chart P

1:1	3:1	5:2 6:18
PERSONAL	DOCTRINAL	PRACTICAL
VINDICATION	EXPOSITION	APPLICATION
testimonial and apologetic	doctrinal and argumentative	practical and hortatory
Lessons 3—6	Lessons 7—8	Lessons 9—10

I. PREPARATION FOR STUDY.

(Note to Bible classes: Because this section of our lesson involves an extra amount of background study, you may want to devote one full unit of study to just this one part.

Such a study of itself will be very interesting and fruitful.)
1. Before analyzing 3:1-24, it will be very helpful to get an overall picture of the general contents of 3:1—5:1. First, mark divisions in your Bible at these points: 3:1, 6, 19, 25; 4:12, 21. Then read the two chapters as you would in survey study, without tarrying over any details. While you make this survey reading, underline in your Bible such things as repeated words and phrases, which are clues to main emphases by Paul.

Proceed in your survey by following study suggestions given below:

a) Were you aware of any *clear* change of content at any point(s) in the section, or did it seem as though Paul is here adding precept upon precept, and argument upon argument, up to the concluding verse? _____

_____

_____

b) Are there any commands or exhortations in the section?

_____

_____

c) Did you observe Paul's use of questions? What is the purpose of this teaching device? _____

_____

_____

d) What man's name appears often in the text? _____
Why would so many references to the Old Testament be made? (Answer this in the light of what Paul is trying to establish in his epistle.) _____

_____

_____

e) What are your overall impressions of this doctrinal section? _____ _____

_____

_____

2. Now that you have surveyed 3:1—5:1 without an out-

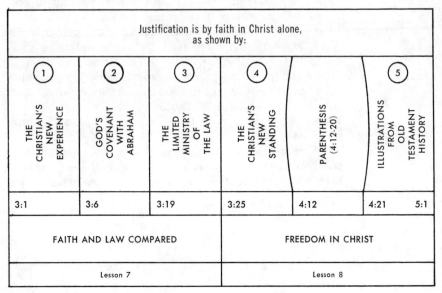

Justification is by faith in Christ alone, as shown by:				

THE CHRISTIAN'S NEW EXPERIENCE ① | GOD'S COVENANT WITH ABRAHAM ② | THE LIMITED MINISTRY OF THE LAW ③ | THE CHRISTIAN'S NEW STANDING ④ | PARENTHESIS (4:12-20) | ILLUSTRATIONS FROM OLD TESTAMENT HISTORY ⑤

3:1 | 3:6 | 3:19 | 3:25 | 4:12 | 4:21 | 5:1

| FAITH AND LAW COMPARED | FREEDOM IN CHRIST |
| Lesson 7 | Lesson 8 |

line in mind, study Chart **Q** and relate its outlines to things you have already seen in your survey.

Observe the following on Chart **Q**:

a) The heading at the top of the chart, beginning with the word "Justification," is the main doctrine which Paul is establishing in the epistle. As an example of this, read 3:24.

b) There is a parenthesis at 4:12-20 where Paul interrupts his exposition by sharing his personal feelings over the problem in the Galatian churches. Read this parenthesis passage again and observe the digression.

c) The passage 3:1—5:1 is divided into two main parts at the bottom of the chart. Relate the outline of points 1-5 to this. (Faith and Law Compared; Freedom in Christ.)

d) Note on the chart that no new section is shown to begin at 4:1. The reason for this will be seen in Lesson 8.

3. Because Abraham is a key person in the passage of this lesson, it will be helpful to read some Old Testament passages which are the background to Paul's reference to him.[1] These passages are listed on Chart R. (Old Testament verses of other background, and some New Testament

---

[1] Cross-reference help like this is a good feature of such Bibles as the Amplified Bible.

Galatians	Old Testament	New Testament
3:6	Gen 15:6[2]	Ro 4:3, 18-22
3:8	Gen 12:1-8	Heb 11:8-10
3:10	Deu 27:26	
3:11	Hab 2:4	Ro 1:17; Heb 10:38
3:12	Lev 18:5	Lk 10:25-28
3:13	Deu 21:23	
3:15-18	Gen 17:1-19	
3:17	Ex 20—23 Ex 12:40	

verses, are also included in this list.) First read the Galatians passage, then the background verses.

II. ANALYSIS.

Segment to be analyzed: 3:1-24.
Paragraph divisions: at verses 1, 6, 10, 13, 15, 19. (Mark these paragraph divisions in your Bible.)

Keep in mind as you study this segment that Paul's main burden in the epistle is to show that *salvation of a sinner is by faith in Christ alone.* Since the Judaizers were upsetting the Galatian Christians by a legalistic formula embracing *law* (salvation equals faith plus law), Paul devotes much of this part of his letter to evaluate the place of faith and of law in the experience of a sinner who turns to Christ for salvation.

A. The Christian's New Experience: 3:1-5.

1. How does this paragraph serve as an introduction to the whole section of 3:1—5:1? (Recall your survey of the earlier part of this lesson.) _____

2. How does Paul refer specifically to the problem at hand? _____

[2] This verse was described by Luther as "the great text of Genesis."

3. What do the words "O foolish Galatians" tell you? ___

_____

Compare these words with the tender address "brethren" of verse 15.

4. How many questions appear in the paragraph? _____

What answer does Paul expect in each case? _____

_____

_____

_____

_____

Would it have been difficult for the Galatian readers to give

correct answers to these questions? _____

5. What contrasts are made here? _____

_____

6. How often does Paul refer to the Spirit? _____
Does each reference have to do with a spiritual _experience_ of the Galatians from the time of their conversion? What point is Paul trying to drive home in that respect? (Cf.

Gal 4:6; 5:18; Eph 1:13.) _____

_____

_____

7. Read verse 1 again. What is the impact of these strong

words: "foolish," "bewitched," "not obey the truth"? ___

_____

Why did Paul refer here to Christ's crucifixion? _____

_____

8. Read verse 2. When does a sinner receive the Spirit?

_____

_____

9. Read verse 3. Compare "having begun" and "now made perfect." _____

_____

What is Paul's logic in this verse? _____

_____

How is this one of Paul's answers to the Judaizers' formula, salvation equals *faith* plus *works*? _____

_____

10. What do you think verse 4 refers to? _____

_____

11. Read verse 5. What spiritual experience is meant here?

_____

_____

What is Paul's repeated point? _____

_____

B. God's Covenant with Abraham: 3:6-18.

1. THE PASSAGE AS A WHOLE.
This passage is a good example of how Old Testament history is vitally contemporary when its types, symbols and other timeless, universal principles are recognized. We should apply this passage to our own day, even as Paul did almost two thousand years ago.

For your analysis, first read the three paragraphs to observe highlights and repeated thoughts. In this segment, repeated words are strong clues to the main point of each paragraph. Be sure to mark these repetitions in your Bible. Try using a different color for each of these words: faith (and believe); law (and curse); covenant (and promise).

Chart S is a partially completed analytical chart of 3:6-18. You may want to set up your own work sheet on a separate sheet of paper (8½ x 11"), recording your own analytical studies on it before looking too closely at the outlines given on Chart S. Some of the study suggestions given below are already worked out on the chart, and some are not. The important thing in all your study is to do as much analysis as possible on your own. But don't hesitate

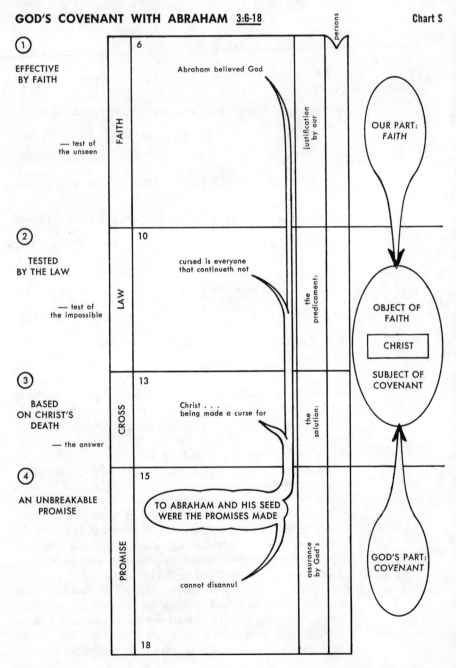

①

**EFFECTIVE
BY FAITH**

— test of
the unseen

FAITH

6

Abraham believed God

justification
by our

persons

OUR PART:
FAITH

②

**TESTED
BY THE LAW**

— test of
the impossible

LAW

10

cursed is everyone
that continueth not

the
predicament:

OBJECT OF
FAITH

CHRIST

SUBJECT OF
COVENANT

③

**BASED
ON CHRIST'S
DEATH**

— the answer

CROSS

13

Christ . . .
being made a curse for

the
solution:

④

**AN UNBREAKABLE
PROMISE**

PROMISE

15

TO ABRAHAM AND HIS SEED
WERE THE PROMISES MADE

cannot disannul

assurance
by God's

GOD'S PART:
COVENANT

18

to use any extra helps to keep up your momentum. If you ever seem to get bogged down in any phase of Bible study, move on to the next phase. All Bible study can and should be dynamic, not static.

What persons are mentioned in the segment? Record this in the narrow right-hand column. What is a main subject of each paragraph? Compare your answers with those of the narrow left-hand column. Where references to Christ are made, what is the point in each case? What is Christ's part in our salvation? What is our part? What is God's part? Complete the study which begins on the chart with, "justification by our _____."

Study the main topical study shown on the chart:

> Key center: "to Abraham and his seed were
> the promises made"
> Master title: *God's Covenant with Abraham*
> Paragraph points: 1. Effective by Faith
> 2. Tested by the Law
> 3. Based on Christ's Death
> 4. An Unbreakable Promise

What phrase in each paragraph is the basis for each of the four paragraph points? Try making your own main topical study with this master title: *Christ's Death.*

2. PARAGRAPH BY PARAGRAPH.

a) Effective by Faith: 3:6-9. What was Abraham's test, in the setting of Genesis 15:6? _____

_____

What does this paragraph teach about the following:

(1) how people were saved in Old Testament days _____

_____

(2) whether non-Jews of Old Testament days could be saved _____

_____

(3) the meaning of justification (vv. 6, 8) _____

_____

(4) the "gospel unto Abraham" _____

_____

(5) a Christian's relationship to Abraham _____

Compare this paragraph with Romans 4:9-12 and James 2:21-26. _____

b) *Tested by the Law*: 3:10-12. Relate the fact of "curse" to the phrase "continueth not" (3:10). _____

What evidence does Paul cite in verse 11 to support his argument? _____

Consult a modern version for a translation of the Habakkuk 2:4 quote of this verse. Compare this reading of 3:12 with that of the King James: "The law, however, is not based on faith but on works; its principle is: 'He who *does* them will live by them'" (Bruce's *Expanded Paraphrase*).

c) *Based on Christ's Death*: 3:13-14. Why did Jesus die?

_____

What is meant by the word "redeemed"? _____

_____

Why did Paul refer to Gentiles only, in verse 14? _____

d) *An Unbreakable Promise*: 3:15-18. Note that the word "seed" is used in a collective sense in the background passages of Genesis 12:1-3, 7; 13:14-17; 17:1-19.[3] Yet, Paul here derives a teaching from the fact that the word "seed"

is singular, not plural. What is his point? _____

_____

Are his interpretation and application justifiable? _____

_____

[3] For example, the Berkeley Version translates "seed" as "descendants." The Amplified Bible uses a collective singular noun, "posterity."

What is meant by the phrase, "the covenant, that was confirmed before of God in Christ" (3:17)? _____

According to this paragraph, which is more enduring, law or promise? What is the *time* aspect of each of these? _____

C. The Limited Ministry of the Law: 3:19-24.

Paul anticipates the obvious question which his readers would make at this point: "Why was the Law given, then?" (3:19, TEV).

The next verses are Paul's answers. Compare each verse of your Bible with that of a modern translation, or a paraphrase (e.g., Living NT). Then record in your own words what the verses show concerning the limited, though important, ministry of the law. 3:19a (cf. Ro 5:20) _____

3:19b-20 _____

3:21 _____

3:22 _____

3:23 _____

3:24 _____

Summarize in your own words what Paul is teaching in this paragraph about the law of God. _____

III. NOTES.

1. "The law is not of faith" (3:12). Literally, this could be translated "The law is not out of faith," that is, it does not start on a principle of faith.

2. "The man that doeth them [laws of God] shall live in them" (3:12). "Under law, one must *do* before he can *live* (Lev 18:5). Under the Gospel one gets life from God through faith, then begins to do the will of God in the energy of that faith."[4]

3. "The promise of the Spirit" (3:14). This is the *promised Spirit*. Prophecies of His future ministry appear in such passages as Ezekiel 36:27; Joel 2:28; Acts 1:5. The fulfillment commenced at Pentecost, Acts 2.

4. "Mediator" (3:20). God gave the *law* to man through mediators: angels and Moses. In the giving of *promise*, there were not two contracting parties. "There is nothing of the nature of a stipulation. The giver is everything, the recipient nothing."[5] But though mediation of the law is a mark of its inferiority, we are not to belittle all situations of mediatorship. Harrison writes, "The mediation of Christ in the present dispensation is not thereby labeled as inferior, for he is not a third party between God and men. God was in Christ reconciling the world."[6]

5. "Schoolmaster" (3:24). The Greek word is *paidagogos* ("child-leader"), from which comes our English word "pedagogue." (The same word appears in 1 Co 4:15.) We may learn what Paul meant by applying this analogy to the law from a description of a *paidagogos* in his day:

> It describes a trusted slave in ancient families of the better class who conducted the children of the family to and from school. He had this supervision over them between the ages of seven and seventeen, and he guarded them from evil society and immoral influences.[7]

The application of this analogy to the law is that its function is discharged "when it conducts us to Christ and leaves us with Him, not merely to receive instruction, but, above all, to receive redemption, which carries with it full sonship."[8]

[4] Everett F. Harrison "*The Epistle to the Galatians,*" p. 1291.
[5] F. Davidson, *The New Bible Commentary*, p. 1008.
[6] Harrison, p. 1292.
[7] Davidson, p. 1008.
[8] Ibid.

IV. FOR THOUGHT AND DISCUSSION.

1. It has been said that "a low view of law leads to legalism in religion; a high view of law makes a man a seeker after grace." If you are studying in a group, discuss this important subject of the function of the law of God. Think about such questions as these:

a) Did the law fulfill its function for anyone in Old Testament days?

b) After a person living during the Old Testament law era came to a saving knowledge of God through faith, what was his attitude to God's laws?

c) How do you think Old Testament saints felt about making offerings to God (for example, the animal offerings of Leviticus), in their intimate faith walk with the Lord? What would such offerings remind them of?

d) Do Old Testament laws have a function today? If so, what is it, for unbelievers, and for Christians?

2. Paul writes in Galatians 3:13 that Christ was made "a curse for us" or "a curse on our behalf." Why was *substitutionary atonement* necessary? (Cf. Jn 11:50; 2 Co 5:21.)

V. FURTHER STUDY.

Study this interesting observation which appears in the Amplified Bible as a footnote to Habakkuk 2:4:

> There is a curious passage in the Talmud [the body of Jewish civil and religious law], which says that in the Law Moses gave six hundred injunctions to the Israelites. As these might prove too numerous to commit to memory,
> David brought them down to eleven in Psalm 15.
> Isaiah reduced these eleven to six in . . . 33:15.
> Micah (6:8) further reduced them to three; and
> Isaiah (56:1) once more brought them down, to two.
> These two Amos (5:4) reduced to one.
> But lest it might be supposed from this that God could be found in the fulfillment of the law only,
> Habakkuk (2:4) said,
> "The just shall live by his faith."[9]

VI. WORDS TO PONDER.

> The way of the law . . . says that a man is saved by obeying every law of God, without one slip. But Christ has bought us out from under the doom of that impossible system by taking the curse for our wrongdoing upon himself" (3:12b-13a, Living Bible).

[9] The quotation is credited to William H. Saulez in *The Romance of the Hebrew Language* (1913).

Freedom in Christ

HAVING DISCUSSED THE SUBJECT OF

GOD'S LAW, PAUL NOW TURNS TO

THE FREEDOM OF THE CHRISTIANS.

The apostle never suggests in any of his writings that God's law and Christian freedom are contradictory or unmixable. One example may be cited from the text of this lesson, relating its concluding verse (5:1) to the last verse of the previous lesson (3:24). The relationship is shown by the following diagram:

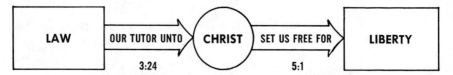

LAW	OUR TUTOR UNTO	CHRIST	SET US FREE FOR	LIBERTY
	3:24		5:1	

The Jewish agitators in the Galatian churches were luring the new Gentile converts back to the yoke of legalistic bondage. Paul's purpose at this point in his letter was to show the Galatians that their newfound emancipation from the law brought them into a new and intimate relationship to God, through His dear Son.

You will find the passage of this lesson to be a very bright one, in view of the nature of its subject.

I. PREPARATION FOR STUDY.

1. Review the survey shown on Chart Q. Chart T is adapted from that overview:
2. For background to the allegory of 4:21-31, read Genesis 16:1-16 and 21:9-21. Also read Isaiah 54:1, which is quoted in Galatians 4:27.

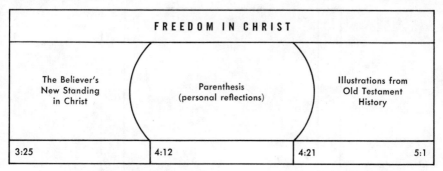

FREEDOM IN CHRIST		
The Believer's New Standing in Christ	Parenthesis (personal reflections)	Illustrations from Old Testament History
3:25	4:12 4:21	5:1

II. ANALYSIS.

Segments to be analyzed: 3:25—4:11; 4:12-20; 4:21—5:1.
Paragraph divisions: at verses 3:25; 4:1, 8, 12, 21.

A. The Believer's New Standing in Christ: 3:25—4:11.

After you have marked the paragraph divisions in your Bible, read this segment first for general impressions and key words. Scan through the segment again and mark every reference to believers in their new standing in Christ (e.g., "children of God," 3:26). Record these on the work sheet of Chart U. Keep on adding to this analytical chart as you continue your study.

1. CHILDREN OF GOD: 3:25-29.
Note the opening word, "but." Compare verse 25 and verse 23. Observe the time references:

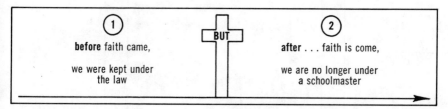

①	**BUT**	②
before faith came,		**after** . . . faith is come,
we were kept under the law		we are no longer under a schoolmaster

Where were the Galatians located on this time line when Paul wrote this letter?

How does each of the following phrases describe a Christian today:

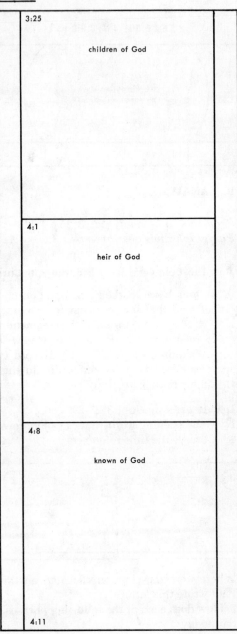

3:25

children of God

4:1

heir of God

4:8

known of God

4:11

"children of God" (v. 26) _____

"baptized in Christ" (v. 27) _____

"have put on Christ" (v. 27; cf. Ro 13:14) _____

"all one in Christ Jesus" (v. 28) _____

"Christ's" (v. 29) _____

"Abraham's seed" (v. 29) _____

"heirs according to the promise" (v. 29) _____

2. HEIR OF GOD: 4:1-7.
What was the position or function of each of these in Paul's day:

heir (4:1) _____

child _____

servant _____

lord _____

tutors (4:2) _____

governors (stewards) _____

father _____

sons (4:5) _____
Complete the following:

ANALOGY (4:1-2)	APPLICATION (4:3-4)
child-heir	
under tutors and governors	
until the time appointed	
of the father	

How much of the gospel is taught in 4:4-5? _____

_____

_____

_____

On "fulness of the time," compare Ephesians 1:10. What is the difference between "children" (v. 3) and "sons" (v. 5)? _____

What is suggested by the phrase, "adoption of sons"? Compare John 8:44. One writer says this is "not sonship, but sonship *conferred*."

What is Paul teaching in verse 6? _____
How does verse 7 summarize the main point of this paragraph? _____

_____

_____

3. KNOWN OF GOD: 4:8-11.
The word "then" of 4:8 may be translated "in the past." How is this verse contrasted with 4:9? _____

What is meant by "weak and beggarly elements" (4:9)? (Cf. 4:10 and 4:3.) _____

Why does Paul extend his reference "ye have known God" to the loftier and greater "are known of God" (4:9)? (Cf. Nah 1:7; Jn 10:14, 27; 1 Co 8:3; 2 Ti 2:19.) _____

_____

_____

B. Parenthesis: 4:12-20.

1. Before writing more about the believer's freedom in Christ (4:21—5:1), Paul pauses at this point to share some of his personal reflections over the problem at hand. This is why we may consider this as a *parenthesis* in the structure of his epistle. Similar digressions appear from time to time in other of his letters. Note the tone of tenderness and pathos as you read the paragraph. Do you think Paul's words in 4:11 brought on this reflective mood

at this point? _____

2. Compare the contents of these two parts of the paragraph:

4:12-15 _____

4:16-20 _____

3. What do you think Paul was referring to by "my temptation which was in my flesh" (4:14)? (See *Notes*.) _____

_____

_____

4. Check the reading of 4:17 in a modern translation.

5. Compare the last phrase of 4:20 with 4:11. _____

_____

_____

ALLEGORY OF GALATIANS 4:21-31
Chart V

HAGAR	SARAH
Old covenant (law)	New covenant (grace)
Mount Sinai	Mount Calvary
Bondage (children as slaves performing the rites of the Sinaitic law)	Freedom
Jerusalem that now is	Heavenly Jerusalem (cf. Heb 12:18-24)
Bondwoman	Freewoman
After the flesh	Divine promise
Her children born into slavery	Her children born into freedom
Powerless to change their status	Dignity of sons with a perferred status
Works	Faith

79

C. Illustrations from Old Testament History: 4:21—5:1.

1. As you read this paragraph, mark every appearance of the word "free." Do the same for the compound names beginning with "bond" (e.g., "bondmaid").

2. What two things is Paul contrasting in this paragraph?

_____

_____

In what verses does he make spiritual applications? _____

_____

3. Study Chart V which shows the contrasts of the allegory of this paragraph.[1] Be sure you have first read the Old Testament background passages cited in *Preparation for Study*. Look in the Bible text for each item listed in the chart.

4. What is Paul's concluding appeal of 5:1? _____

_____

_____

5. For a summary exercise, study Chart W, which shows the highlights of this lesson.

III. NOTES.

1. "In bondage under the elements of the world" (4:3). Some interpret these "elements" as being those of the physical world (2 Pe 3:10, 12). Others see them as "ruling spirits of the universe" (TEV). It is more likely that the reference is to the rudiments of legalistic Judaism. This is supported by the reappearance of the same word in 4:9, followed immediately by examples of legalistic rules and customs (4:10).

2. "Made of a woman" (4:4). This phrase emphasizes the real *humanity* of Jesus.

3. "Made under the law" (4:4). That is, Jesus was born and raised under the Jewish law. For example, He was circumcised, presented in the temple to God, and reared

---

[1] This chart is from Merrill F. Unger, *Unger's Bible Handbook*, p. 666.

Jer 31:33, "Law in their inward parts"

L A W   **S P I R I T**

"We were kept in custody
under the law"
3:23 (NASB)

"Baptized into Christ"
3:27

SLAVES (4:7)   SONS AND HEIRS (4:7)

G O D ' S   T I M E T A B L E

Law is good,
but it was for this
era

Fullness of time
(4:4)

in a devout Jewish home. "It was necessary that he keep the Law perfectly in order to redeem his people from the bondage and curse of the Law."[2]

4. "Abba, Father" (4:6). The original text retained the Aramaic word *Abba* and translated it into the Greek ("Father"). The word appears in two other places in the New Testament: Mark 14:36; Romans 8:15. It was an intimate word of the Palestinian household, on the lips of a child addressing its father. The spiritual implications of this fact are tremendous.

5. "My temptation which was in my flesh" (4:14). Most Bible versions identify the temptation (trial) as being the Galatian Christians'. For example, "that which was a trial to you in my bodily condition you did not despise or loathe, but you received me as an angel of God, as Christ

---

[2] Everett F. Harrison, "The Epistle to the Galatians," p. 1293.

81

Jesus Himself" (NASB). One can only speculate on Paul's physical weakness or disease. Some views suggested are: malaria, eye disease, epilepsy. Some expositors relate 2 Corinthians 12:7 to this infirmity.

6. "Ye would have plucked out your own eyes" (4:15). This is probably not an indirect reference to Paul's infirmity of 4:14. The eye symbolizes one's most precious physical possession, and Paul is probably recognizing by this analogy the hitherto intense devotion of his Galatian converts to himself.

IV.   FOR THOUGHT AND DISCUSSION.

1. What is the difference between liberty and license? Does the New Testament teaching on Christian liberty endorse the do-as-you-please attitude? Can you think of any verses that support your answer?

2. Are there boundaries and limitations in this Christian freedom? If so, what are they?

3. Is the phrase "stand fast . . . in" of 5:1 a suggestion of boundary in Christian living? What about the common New Testament phrase, "in Christ"?

4. What is so significant about your privilege as a child of God to address Him, as Christ did, "Abba"? How much are you aware of this intimate relationship when you talk to God in prayer? How can it be nurtured?

V. FURTHER STUDY.

Study the doctrine of adoption as it is taught in the New Testament. (A concordance will direct you to the few though important references.)

VI.   WORDS TO PONDER.

I once was an outcast stranger on earth,
A sinner by choice, and an alien by birth;
But I've been adopted, my name's written down,
An heir to a mansion, a robe, and a crown.
I'm a child of the King, a child of the King;
With Jesus my Saviour, I'm a child of the king.

Harriet E. Buell

The New Walk of Christians

PAUL MOVES TO THE PRACTICAL AND

CONCLUDING PART OF HIS LETTER,

ON THE CHRISTIAN'S DAILY WALK.

Here his appeal is to action—putting the gospel to work in everyday living. The applications are naturally in the setting of the main problem being discussed in the epistle —whether or not a Christian is still in bondage to God's law after his conversion.

Chart X is a review survey of the epistle to show the context of the passage of these next two lessons.

CONTEXT OF CHAPTERS 5 AND 6   Chart X

1:1	3:1	5:2 6:18
PERSONAL	DOCTRINAL	PRACTICAL
APPEAL TO REASON	APPEAL TO CHOICE	APPEAL TO ACTION
source of the gospel (1:11)	bondage or freedom law or faith	fruit of the Spirit (5:22)

I. PREPARATION FOR STUDY.

1. Recall from your study of previous lessons that Paul did not write that God's law is evil. What he did consider

evil was a Christian's return to the bondage of the law, thus forfeiting the blessings of freedom in Christ (5:1).

2. Since a key word of the passage of our present lesson is "Spirit," it is helpful to compare the ministries of the Spirit and of the law as related to the event of Christ in world history. One such comparison is shown below. Try thinking of other ways to compare these.

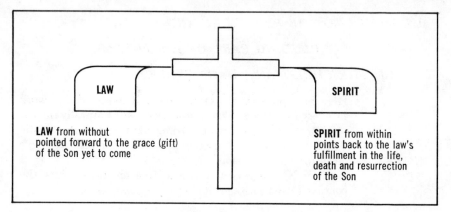

LAW from without
pointed forward to the grace (gift)
of the Son yet to come

SPIRIT from within
points back to the law's
fulfillment in the life,
death and resurrection
of the Son

3. Note that we are considering 5:2 rather than 5:1 as the opening verse of this segment. Actually, 5:1 is a transitional verse, that is, a conclusion to the previous passage (3:25—5:1), *and* an introduction to this passage (5:1-26). Read 5:1 again, and keep in the back of your mind that this verse is an essential part of Paul's appeals in chapter 5. (For example, note the command of the first three words of 5:1.)

II. ANALYSIS.

Segment to be analyzed: 5:2-26.
Paragraph divisions: at verses 2, 7, 13, 16.

A. The Segment as a Whole.

1. Mark the paragraph divisions in your Bible; then read the passage once for major impressions. Underline repeated words and key phrases. Record these on the work sheet of Chart Y.

2. What is the main point of each paragraph? Record this and other observations on the chart.

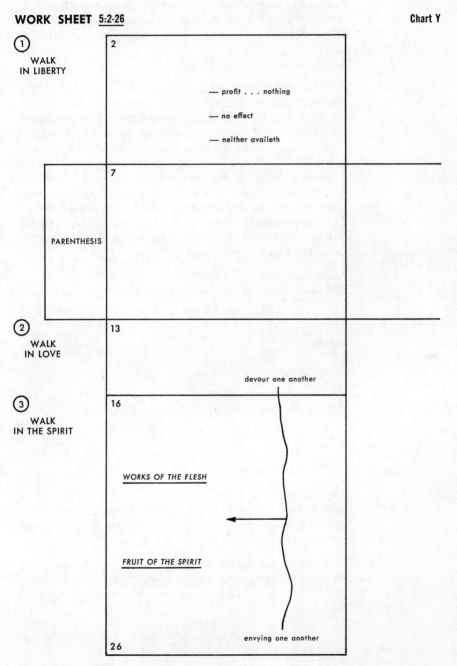

① WALK
IN LIBERTY

2

— profit . . . nothing

— no effect

— neither availeth

7

PARENTHESIS

② WALK
IN LOVE

13

③ WALK
IN THE SPIRIT

16

devour one another

WORKS OF THE FLESH

FRUIT OF THE SPIRIT

envying one another

26

3. In what way is the paragraph 5:7-12 a parenthesis in Paul's exposition of 4:12-20? Compare this with the earlier parenthesis. Are the subjects and tones similar?

B. Paragraph by Paragraph.

1. WALK IN LIBERTY: 5:2-6.
A specific reference to this liberty appeared in the preceding verse, 5:1. Do you see any suggestion in this paragraph that Paul is still thinking about this subject of freedom? (For example, what does the word "debtor," v. 3, suggest to you?)

Make a study of the three subjects of *faith, hope* and *love* as these appear in verses 5-6. Read these other passages where the three jewels are brought together: 1 Thessalonians 1:3; Romans 5:1-5; 1 Corinthians 13:13; Colossians 1:4-5. On love, compare Romans 13:9-10; Leviticus 19:18.

2. PARENTHESIS: 5:7-12.
How does Paul use each of the following in this paragraph:

reason: _____

persuasion: _____

encouragement: _____

3. WALK IN LOVE: 5:13-15.
What does Paul teach here about the following:

liberty _____

license _____

love _____

Note the repetition of the phrase "one another." The phrase appears again in verse 26. Keep this in mind for an exercise that appears later.

4. WALK IN THE SPIRIT: 5:16-26.
Note every appearance of the word "Spirit" in the paragraph. How is the Spirit compared with the flesh (5:17)?

_____

_____

What is meant here by "flesh"? _____

_____

How is the Spirit compared with the law (5:18)? _____

_____

What practical truth in Christian living is suggested by the picture word "walk" (5:16)? See Romans 6:4; 8:4; 1 Corinthians 3:3; Ephesians 4:1, 17; Philippians 3:18.

_____

_____

What is meant by the key phrase, "Walk in the Spirit" (5:16)? Relate this to the following:

a) fulfilling the lust of the flesh (5:16) _____

_____

b) fruit of the Spirit (5:22-23) _____

_____

c) life in the Spirit (5:25) _____

_____

Study carefully the two important lists appearing in the paragraph. Do you see any *groupings* in the lists? Record the two lists to help in your study.

Works of the Flesh (5:19-21)	Fruit of the Spirit (5:22-23)

How many sins of strife are listed among the works of the flesh? Relate this to each of the following two verses: 5:15

and 5:26. _____

_____

III. NOTES.

1. "If ye be circumcised, Christ shall profit you nothing" (5:2). *The Living Bible* paraphrases Paul's intention here: "If you [Gentiles] are counting on circumcision and keeping the Jewish laws to make you right with God, then Christ cannot save you."

2. "I would they were even cut off" (5:12). The New American Standard Bible translates the last phrase as "mutilate themselves." Paul may have been thinking of the rite of castration to which pagan priests submitted themselves in devotion to their gods. *The Wycliffe Bible Commentary* represents Paul's intention thus: "As an emasculated man has lost the power of propagation, so should these agitators be reduced to impotence in spreading their false doctrine."[1]

3. "Walk in the Spirit" (5:16). Many versions translate this phrase as "Walk by the Spirit." TEV paraphrases, "Let the Spirit direct your lives."

4. "Witchcraft" (5:20). This is sorcery, or magic performed with the aid of evil spirits. The Greek word translated "witchcraft" is *pharmakia* (cf. the English "pharmacy"), and appears in such New Testament verses as Revelation 9:21; 18:23. "In sorcery, the use of drugs, whether simple or potent, was generally accompanied by incantations and appeals to occult powers."[2]

5. "Fruit of the Spirit" (5:22). Paul here intentionally chose the singular word "fruit" over the plural "fruits" (cf. Ja 3:17). Among other things this suggests a unity of this spiritual cluster of Christian virtues, all of them originating in Christ and manifested in the power of the Spirit.

[1] Everett F. Harrison, "The Epistle to the Galatians," p. 1295.
[2] W. E. Vine, *An Expository Dictionary of New Testament Words*, 4:52.

IV. FOR THOUGHT AND DISCUSSION.

1. How does love guard against a Christian's abuse of his freedom in Christ?
2. How is the Holy Spirit a Guide in the exercise of Christian liberty?
3. What is the insecurity of any legalistic creed or religion?
4. What are the two natures in a Christian, always warring against each other? (Cf. 5:16-17.) What determines which nature is victor in any particular conflict?
5. "They that are Christ's have crucified the flesh" (5:24). What is meant by this? How is such a crucifixion accomplished in a Christian's life? Study Romans 6:5-11 in this connection.

V. FURTHER STUDY.

With the help of a concordance read the various verses in the New Testament where the words of the two lists of this passage (5:19-21 and 5:22-23) appear. These verses will throw further light on the meaning of the words.

VI. WORDS TO PONDER.

If the Spirit is the source of our life, let the Spirit also direct our course (5:25, NEB).

Obligations
Attend Christian Liberty

CHRISTIAN LIBERTY IS NOT WITHOUT

OBLIGATIONS AND RESPONSIBILITIES,

AS PAUL CLEARLY MAINTAINS HERE.

The chapter includes a variety of thoughts which Paul wanted to share with his Galatian readers before penning the final "Amen." There is an informality about the passage which relieves the intensity and sharpness of the earlier chapters, and yet Paul does not relent even here in his criticism of the Jewish-Christian agitators in Galatia. His last words before the benediction reveal how sorely this problem had vexed him:

> Let no one give me any more trouble; for the scars
> I have on my body show that I am the slave of Jesus
> (6:17, TEV).

I. PREPARATION FOR STUDY.

You may want to set up a work sheet (on 8½ x 11″ paper) similar to the one shown as Chart Z. Use this analytical chart to record your various observations and interpretations as you study.

II. ANALYSIS.

Segment to be analyzed: 6:1-18.
Paragraph divisions: at verses 1, 6, 11, 12, 17, 18.

A. The Segment as a Whole.

Read the passage as you have done in previous lessons. Consult modern translations or paraphrases to clarify any verses in this segment (e.g., 6:4). What is the main point of each paragraph? Compare your conclusions with the

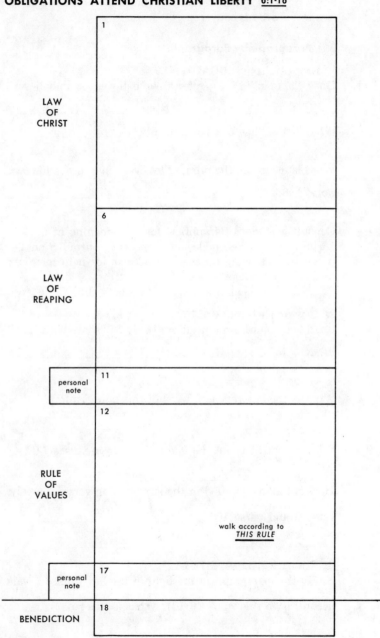

LAW
OF
CHRIST

1

6

LAW
OF
REAPING

personal
note

11

12

RULE
OF
VALUES

walk according to
THIS RULE

personal
note

17

18

BENEDICTION

outline shown on Chart Z. Verses 11 and 17 are personal notes by Paul which reveal how much he had suffered in ministering to his converts.

B. Paragraph by Paragraph.

1. LAW OF CHRIST: 6:1-5.
Does "a man" (6:1) refer to a believer or unbeliever?

_____

What is the "law of Christ" of 6:2? _____

_____

What is meant by the phrase "let every man prove his own work" (6:4)? _____

_____

Consult a modern paraphrase for the meaning of 6:4*b*.
   How do you reconcile the *apparent* contradiction between the following phrases (see *Notes* for help in this):
   "Bear ye one another's burdens" (6:2)
   "Every man shall bear his own burden" (6:5).

2. LAW OF REAPING: 6:6-10.
Read "communicate unto him" (6:6) as "share with him."
What is to be shared? _____

_____

What is the key repeated word of this paragraph? _____

_____

What is taught about the *law of reaping* in verses 7-9? ___

_____

How is the law applied in the surrounding verses, namely, verse 6 and verse 10? _____

_____

3. RULE OF VALUES: 6:12-16.
Study this paragraph in the light of the key phrase, "walk according to this rule" (6:16). What is this rule? _____

_____

What false values does Paul write about in this paragraph?

_____

_____

Why do you think Paul added the phrase "and upon the Israel of God" (6:16) in view of the main theme of the epistle? _____

_____

4. BENEDICTION: 6:18.
What is significant about the two words "brethren" and "grace" in view of what Paul has written to the Galatians?

_____

_____

III. NOTES.

1. "Ye which are spiritual" (6:1). Compare 1 Peter 2:5.
2. "One another's burdens" (6:2); "his own burden" (6:5). Two different kinds of burdens are referred to here. The first translates the Greek *baros*, meaning a heavy weight, used here to represent the cares, sorrows and tribulations of life. Christians are to help carry the load of these burdens which weigh down fellow Christians. The second word "burden" (6:5) translates the Greek *phortion*, which was something to be borne, not necessarily a heavy object. One example of the use of this word in the first century was for a bill or invoice for a property tax. If Paul was using the word in this sense, he may have been thinking of that which a Christian must bear at the judgment seat of Christ, for unacceptable deeds done in the flesh as a Christian. (Cf. Ro 14:12; 1 Co 3:10-15.) This interpretation recognizes a close connection between 6:4 and 6:5. Of this Harrison writes in *The Wycliffe Bible Commentary*:

> Each [Christian] had better evaluate himself aright now, in preparation for the Lord's judgment of him in the coming day, when he must **bear his own burden.** He will be held responsible for his own life and work (Ro 14:12).[1]

[1] Everett F. Harrison, "The Epistle to the Galatians," p. 1297.

The bright truth in connection with this coming judgment is that Christ offers to help Christians *now* to build with that which will survive the fire of judgment (1 Co 3:14). In this connection also it is interesting to notice that Jesus used the word *phortion* (burden) in His invitation to souls burdened with the sin problem: "Come to Me all you who labor and are heavily burdened [*phortion*], and I will give you rest. Take My yoke upon you . . . for My yoke is easy and My burden [*phortion*] is light" (Mt 11:28-30, New Berkeley).

IV. FOR THOUGHT AND DISCUSSION.

This is the appropriate time for a final review of your study of Galatians. On the basis of that study, make a list of at least twenty practical lessons taught by this epistle. Look for three to four such lessons in each chapter. If you are studying in a group, it will be very helpful for the members to share their lists.

V. FURTHER STUDY.

The epistle of James is in many ways a companion to Galatians, since both are about *works* in the Christian's life. You may want to study James as your next Bible-study project, now that Galatians is fresh in your mind.

VI. PAUL'S CONCLUDING BENEDICTION.

Brethren, the grace of our Lord Jesus Christ be with your spirit. Amen (6:18).

This is the Apostle's farewell. He ends his Epistle as he began by wishing the Galatians the grace of God. We can hear him say: "I have presented Christ to you, I have pleaded with you, I have reproved you, I have overlooked nothing that I thought might be of benefit to you. All I can do now is to pray that our Lord Jesus Christ would bless my Epistle and grant you the guidance of the Holy Ghost.[2]

[2] Martin Luther, *A Commentary on St. Paul's Epistle to the Galatians*, p. 282.

Appendix

The North Galatian and South Galatian Views

In Paul's day the term *Galatia* had two connotations. One was ethnic, and the other was provincial. A summary of the historical background will explain the reason for the differences:

250 B.C. Migratory Celtic tribes (Gauls) moved in from the west and north, settling down in Asia Minor, mostly in the northern half.

189 B.C. The people were conquered by the Romans.

25 B.C. Augustus made the region a Roman province, calling it Galatia (after "Gaul").

A.D. 41 The original boundaries were extended southward to include such cities as Derbe and surrounding areas.

Here are the two views and some arguments that are advanced to defend each:

I. "CHURCHES OF GALATIA" WERE CHURCHES IN THE NORTHERN REGIONS.

1. This is "ethnic" Galatia, using the term in a *popular* sense.
2. The churches were founded on Paul's second or third missionary journey (e.g., Ac 16:6; 18:23).
3. This area was the true Galatia, as to race and language.
4. There were more Gentiles in the northern cities, hence the problem referred to in Galatians would more likely exist there.
5. This was the view generally held by the church in early centuries.

95

II. "CHURCHES OF GALATIA" WERE CHURCHES IN THE SOUTHERN REGIONS.

1. This is "provincial" Galatia, using the term in an *official* sense.
2. The churches were founded on Paul's first missionary journey (Ac 13—14).
3. We know of no churches existing at this early date in the northern parts of Galatia.
4. Barnabas, who accompanied Paul on the first journey but not on the second, is mentioned more than once in Galatians 2, as if he were well known to the readers (2:1, 9, 13).
5. The letter was written *before* the Jerusalem council (Ac 15), and therefore before the second missionary journey, or Paul would surely have referred to the council's decree favoring Gentile Christian freedom from the Mosaic law, which is the main problem being addressed in Galatians.
6. This is the view generally held today.

Moody Press, a ministry of the Moody Bible Institute, is designed for education, evangelization and edification. If we may assist you in knowing more about Christ and the Christian life, please write us without obligation to: Moody Press, c/o MLM, Chicago, Illinois 60610.